SURVIVAL TO THRIVAL

BUILDING THE
ENTERPRISE STARTUP

BOOK 2: CHANGE OR BE CHANGED

Survival to Thrival: Building the Enterprise Startup
Book 2: Change or Be Changed

For more information, please contact:
Mascot Books
620 Herndon Parkway #320
Herndon, VA 20170
info@mascotbooks.com

CPSIA Code: PRFRE0119A
Library of Congress Control Number: 2018914690
ISBN-13: 978-1-68401-747-8

Illustrations by Steve Raikow and Frances Luu.
Marketing and production by Frances Luu.

Printed in Canada

SURVIVAL to THRIVAL

BUILDING THE ENTERPRISE STARTUP

BOOK 2

CHANGE OR BE CHANGED

BOB TINKER & TAE HEA NAHM

DEDICATION

To Christine, Christian, and Chloe, for your love and patience. You made it possible.

—*Bob*

To Ali, David, and Rosemarie, for your support and being my sounding board.

—*Tae Hea*

SPECIAL ACKNOWLEDGMENTS

Thank you to the dozens and dozens of entrepreneurs, colleagues, and advisors who helped us along our enterprise startup journey.

Experienced CEOs and Entrepreneurs:
Brett Galloway, Craig Johnson, Faizel Lakhani, Joseph Ansanelli, Mark McLaughlin, Phil Fernandez, Rob Meinhardt, and Yuri Pikover

2008 First Time CEO Club:
Rob Goldman, Seth Kenvin, and Tien Tzuo

Our Colleagues:
To the entire team at MobileIron for their teamwork and patience with a first-time CEO. To the Storm team for sharing your battle scars of company building. And, to our investor colleagues and board members: Aaref Hilaly, Frank Marshall, Gaurav Garg, Jim Tolonen, Matt Howard, and the extended team at Foundation, IVP, Norwest, and Sequoia for your coaching, confidence, and experience.

TABLE OF CONTENTS

SURVIVAL TO THRIVAL:
SERIES INTRO

[Note to reader: If you have already read Book 1, skip this series intro]

Entrepreneurship and Silicon Valley have a special ethos: Pay it forward. Entrepreneurs helping entrepreneurs. Peers helping peers. Colleagues helping colleagues. Experienced entrepreneurs sharing advice and battle scars with new entrepreneurs. Our journey was made possible by dozens and dozens of people who helped us along the way. From CEOs who were a couple years ahead of us, to previously successful entrepreneurs, to our admittedly awkward 2008 "First-time CEO Club." Just as important were all of our teammates across our startup journeys who brought their entrepreneurial experience and patience to the table. Every one of these people, and dozens more, contributed and helped on our journey. Some had a vested interest in our success; most did not and simply helped, often for no reason other than karma and simple thanks. The ethos goes back decades:

> *A 13-year-old Steve Jobs called Bill Hewlett (HewlettPackard co-founder and CEO) after finding his phone number in the phone book. "And he picked up the phone, and I talked to him, and I asked him if he'd give me some spare parts for something I was building called a frequency counter, and he did. But in addition to that, he gave me something way more important, he gave me a job that summer...at Hewlett-Packard...and I was in heaven." (Cupertino Patch newspaper, June 8, 2011)*

This book is for you, the enterprise entrepreneur

There are few books focused on enterprise entrepreneurs. We decided to tackle that gap and do our part for the entrepreneurial ethos by writing our two *Survival to Thrival* books.

If you are an entrepreneur, an employee, or an investor anywhere on the enterprise-startup journey, these books are for you. We've written them to provide big-picture frameworks that explain: how things fit together when building an enterprise startup; how to anticipate what's next; the hard lessons we learned (and then unlearned) as the company evolved; what worked and what didn't in tough situations; and things that we saw others do that we wished we had known earlier. And sometimes we just vent about crappy situations for which there is no good answer.

Survival to Thrival: Building an enterprise startup is different

Consumer companies catch a trend just right. They capture zeitgeist in a bottle and accelerate—or they don't, and they die. Enterprise companies don't have magical zeitgeist; they're more systematic. Enterprise buyers are more deliberate. Enterprise startups often have more complex go-to-markets. And they often spend way more time in "survival mode," simply trying not to die while they figure out product and go-to-market. Then at some point—if they're one of the lucky ones—the business accelerates. It no longer becomes about Survival ("How do we not die?") but about what we call "Thrival" ("How do we win?").

Once an enterprise company accelerates and shifts to Thrival mode, everything changes. What used to work no longer works. Demands on the business change. Demands on the leaders change. Get it right, and the enterprise startup becomes a business that matters and creates enormous value. Get it wrong—fail to evolve, fail to change, fail to make the transition to Thrival—and the startup fades into irrelevancy. That's the enterprise journey, from Survival to Thrival.

Why two books?

Traditional business-book publishers want 200-page books. But today's entrepreneurs consume content in smaller chunks, so we decided to ignore the publishers and write two smaller books—of about 120 pages—that can each be read during a single plane flight.

The first book is about the **company journey**: lessons learned across the business, product, go-to-market, and team as a startup grows from the Founding Idea, fighting to survive, all the way through to a thriving sustainable industry leader. The book introduces what we believe is the "missing link" to unlock enterprise growth, Go-To-Market Fit, and marks the transition from Survival to Thrival. The changes along enterprise startup journey are both nerve-racking and breathtaking. Knowing what's coming next is half the battle—as is, ironically, recognizing that what used to work might actually be the exact wrong thing for the next stage. Our hope is that Book 1 helps entrepreneurs succeed now and anticipate what's next for their company.

The second book, *Change or Be Changed*, is about **the people journey**: lessons learned—and unlearned—for CEOs, leadership teams, and boards on their journey from Survival to Thrival. As the company changes, roles change, and people must change, or be changed. At the same time, there is very little institutional knowledge passed down to help startup leaders understand how their jobs change, and therefore how they must change themselves to succeed. Some of what makes people wildly successful in the current stage ironically must be unlearned for the next. **Unlearning is key**. Unlearning is an invigorating and transformational experience, yet painful and turbulent for the team, the CEO and the board. Culture becomes the fabric that holds the team together during the turbulence of unlearning and is the foundation on which startups are built. Like Book 1, we hope Book 2 helps entrepreneurs succeed now and anticipate what's next for themselves and their teams.

Most importantly, both books have the same goal: to help entrepreneurs who are taking this crazy ride, with all of its ups and downs, recognize that they are not alone.

A little bit about us

The "we" is Bob Tinker, a three-time enterprise entrepreneur, and Tae Hea Nahm (pronounced Tay-Hee Naam), a long-time venture capitalist. We spent the last 15 years on the battlefield together as an entrepreneur-investor combo team, and fortunate enough to help build two enterprise startups from zero to high growth, resulting in one acquisition and one IPO. The first, WiFi company Airespace that was bought by Cisco for $450M, and then mobile security company MobileIron that we took public in 2014.

Bob was the founding CEO of MobileIron, an enterprise startup that, in eight years, went from "three people and a whiteboard" to over $150M in annual revenue, over 12,000 enterprise customers, and nearly 1,000 people. As an executive at Airespace, Bob helped accelerate the go-to-market from zero to an $80M run rate. Like most startup CEOs, Bob doesn't really care all that much about general theories. He wants to charge up the hill, knock down problems, bring the team together, and build a great business. He wants to know how to make good decisions, deal with tough issues, and stay one step ahead. In that sense, he is representative of founder-CEOs, who, unlike investors, are fully committed to a single mission and don't have a portfolio to fall back on. Bob likes to cut to the takeaway for the entrepreneur. He is a punchline guy.

Tae Hea is a founding partner at Storm Ventures. He was an investor in and the chairman of MobileIron, and the founding CEO, investor, and board member of Airespace. Previously, as a founding partner of Venture Law Group, he participated in several hundred startup journeys as an attorney and VC. His work resulted in 15 IPOs. Like many Silicon Valley investors, Tae Hea tends to pattern-match for success and failure across his portfolio of investments. He compares a company situation to his prior experience to understand the drivers that predict future outcomes and help the entrepreneur. As an applied-math major in college, he deliberately (sometimes overly) analyzes the startup journey to create and fit a model. He is a model guy.

Even after 15 years of shared experience, reconciling our two different perspectives to write these books was a surprising challenge. We found the process both painful and fascinating, but hope it delivers a better end result for you. If these books help you better capitalize on your opportunity or avoid even a single pothole, then mission accomplished.

Our wish

Building an enterprise startup is a great ride. A scary ride. And sometimes a lonely ride. In the beginning, it's simply about Survival—just trying not to die. With luck and hard work, it becomes about Thrival—your opportunity to build something that matters. No matter what, the journey is an insanely intense learning experience about business, people, and, in the end, yourself. We're all learning every day. For the millions of entrepreneurs around the world who have and will continue to take the plunge to build the next great enterprise company, your journey from Survival to Thrival is an inspiration. Our hats are off to you.

BOOK 2 INTRO:
CHANGE OR BE CHANGED

Book 1 of the *Survival to Thrival* series is about **The Company Journey** from Survival ("Don't die!") to Thrival ("How do we win?"). Book 2, **Change or Be Changed**, is about *you*, the enterprise entrepreneurs, as you make the journey from Survival to Thrival.

Book 2 is about the challenges and changes faced by the enterprise-startup team—the CEO, the leaders, the broader team, and the board. How the team adapts and evolves with the needs of the company is just as critical to a startup's success as evolving product execution or sales execution. These people changes don't get as much attention as the changes a company goes through, but often they are equally challenging and perhaps even more important than the company changes.

The books are not a hero's journey. Rather, the books pull together lessons learned, things that worked, things that didn't work, stuff we wish we had known, and things that just stink as enterprise entrepreneurs struggle to transform a founding Idea into a meaningful company that makes a difference in the world.

Book 1 recap:

- Nailing a **Founding Idea** with gravity to attract people and capital

- Iterating to **Product-Market Fit (PM-Fit)** by overcoming founder bias

- Introducing the new concept of **Go-To-Market Fit (GTM-Fit)**, which is the missing link to unlock growth in an enterprise startup

- Changing mindset in order to accelerate to **Category Leadership**

- Making the turbulent transition to **Sustainable Industry Leadership**

SURVIVAL • THRIVAL

FOUNDING PMF GTM FIT ACCELERATE TO CATEGORY LEADER SUSTAINABLE INDUSTRY LEADER

Don't die
(while finding our path)

How do we win?

The fun and the fear: Change or be changed

If an enterprise startup is fortunate enough to experience success, the nature of the company changes. It has to.

Company changes drive massive role changes. Each new role is often a very different job that requires very different behavior, but, confusingly, it has the same title. Role changes mean the people must change themselves and how they work. These people changes are profound. Everyone in the startup—from the CEO to leaders to individual contributors—must adapt to the new role or, for the good of the mission, be changed. Change or be changed.

Yet, there is little institutional knowledge passed down to startup leaders to help them understand how their jobs change and how they must also change as the startup grows. The leaders are simply left to figure it out, boiling slowly like a frog in a pot, until one day they boil to death. Instead, startup leaders can anticipate the changes in their role and in themselves. While changing yourself is difficult and sometimes painful, it's also a fun and invigorating learning experience.

Everyone must change how they work, change how they interact, and change how they behave. And they must do all that while fighting to survive, and then out-executing the competition to thrive. CEOs struggle to re-conceptualize their roles as the startup's needs change. Today's superstar executives struggle to adapt to tomorrow's needs. The cultural foundation of the company, which seemed immutable in the early days, must adapt and evolve, while at the same time providing a foundation to hold the company together. Questions of business execution, winning performance, loyalty, and culture become intertwined. The team strains under rapid change.

The degree of people change needed is mind-bending. But each change represents a career-building learning opportunity for the team and a chance to make a difference in the business.

The key to success: Unlearning

What makes change so hard? People have a very natural tendency to repeat what worked in the past. For a while, that repetition is great and powerful. But in the enterprise-startup journey, there comes a point when the very behaviors and skills that drive the startup's teams success from A to B become the very obstacles that hold the team back when taking the company from B to C—even going as far as to sometimes kill a promising startup.

Entrepreneurs thrive on learning but typically spend very little time on the equally important unlearning. Unlearning is tricky. Unlearning is counter-intuitive. Leaders must decide what to change and what to retain. Everyone from the CEO to individual

contributors must unlearn some of the behaviors that previously made them successful and learn new ones for the next stage. They must unlearn their old jobs and learn new ones. The entire company must unlearn old successful habits and create new ones.

Unlearning under stress is painfully hard. It feels like rewiring an airplane in flight while fighting desperately to gain altitude. Ripping open the fuselage of an airplane mid-flight to mess with the internal wiring seems like the last thing anybody

would want to do. It's deeply uncomfortable, highly stressful, and sometimes even dangerous. But on the journey from Survival to Thrival, unlearning is essential.

It's about the people

Each challenge and change during the enterprise-startup journey creates pain and risk, but they also represent a growth opportunity for each person and the company. Being part of a team that is learning and unlearning its way to success is inspiring. Creating a culture that simultaneously binds a team together, adapts to change, and transcends any individual is profoundly satisfying. Learning together—and unlearning together—with fellow entrepreneurs and teammates builds deep relationships and camaraderie that will last a lifetime. The people are what make the journey worthwhile.

Survive well. Thrive well. Pass it on and pay it forward.

Good luck!

Bob & Tae Hea

CHAPTER 1:
CEO

The startup CEO is a challenging and sometimes lonely job.

In no other job is the *unlearn* imperative as acute. As an enterprise startup grows, the CEO job evolves—and so must the CEO. Fighting against or denying change risks limiting the company's and CEO's prospects. By embracing the change, the CEO job becomes a spectacular learning experience. The strain of building a company while constantly learning—and unlearning—ages the soul, yet there is good news: the CEO job is a fascinating exercise in self-awareness and personal growth that—like many big things in life—changes a person for the better on the inside.

What does the CEO do?

From the outside, the job of the enterprise-startup CEO looks straightforward—to lead the company and make decisions. But what is the job really? It boils down to three things: figure out the strategy, drive execution, and lead.

Strategy	Execution	Leadership
Paint the vision	Decide what to do & in what sequence	Passion & commitment
Build business value	Decide who does what	Set the culture
Anticipate change	Drive progress	Attract talent, customers, & capital
Respond to the market	Solve problems	Communication & alignment
	Make decisions & tradeoffs	Make big/tough decisions
		Adapt & unlearn
Make Decisions		

What does it feel like? A crazy cacophony of never-ending demands, things to do, issues to deal with, giddy highs, and gut-wrenching lows—all while desperately trying to ensure the startup doesn't die (Survival). Then if the CEO is lucky, the startup unlocks growth and accelerates to market and industry leadership (Thrival).

CEO journey: From micro to macro

More than any other role, the CEO job evolves enormously as the startup grows. It almost feels like three different roles. An analogy for the changes in CEO role is found in comic books and action movies.

CEO Job 1: Captain America/Wonder Woman and Platoon

The CEO leads a small, devoted platoon in the woods, where everyone does battle, throws punches, digs ditches, gets dirty. It's hand-to-hand combat.

CEO Job 2: Captain America and the Avengers

The CEO recruits and leads a band of Avenger superheroes (the executive team), each of whom has a special superpower that makes him/her stronger or better than the CEO in their own special way.

CEO Job 3: Professor X and the X-Men

Like a dean at a university, the CEO leads an army of superheroes, setting the vision and hiring the new teachers who both fight battles and bring up the next generation of talent. The CEO must do fewer things—but for a lot more people, and repeats him/herself a lot.

Each CEO role is very different, and the exact timing of the role shifts varies somewhat. But the picture on the next page provides a rough sense of how the CEO roles map onto the stages of the company journey that we outlined in Book 1—the founding, finding Product-Market Fit, finding Go-To-Market Fit, accelerating to Category Leader, and transcending to Sustainable Industry Leader.

Figure 1: Mapping CEO roles onto the company journey

Many CEOs thrive on execution and learning. However, succeeding in each new CEO role doesn't just require learning, it requires *unlearning*. Unlearning means deliberately (and often counterintuitively) stopping many of the behaviors that allowed the CEO to succeed up until that point—and then relearning a new set of skills and behaviors required for the next CEO role. The changes are often difficult and awkward—and very personal. In addition to reconceptualizing the job, at a very personal level CEOs must reconceptualize how they see themselves adding value. It's harder than it sounds. But the startup's success depends on it. Personal success depends on it.

1] Captain America/Wonder Woman and Platoon: Doing the work

Captain America or Wonder Woman (CA/WW) is a hands-on CEO, in charge of the startup in Survival mode, simply trying not to die.

CA/WW is an *individual contributor* who, with access only to limited resources, does it all: runs through walls, leads the troops into battle, digs ditches, engages in hand-to-hand combat. This might mean doing 150 product demonstrations to internalize customer feedback, or banging out the code for a product while flying cross-country to meet a prospective customer.

CA/WW is the *project manager*. The enterprise startup is one big project, and the CEO is the project manager. Their hands-on approach to each task shortens the time required to make key decisions, ensures tight coordination, and allows small teams to move quickly. Communication is seldom a critical problem at this stage. The hands-on approach triggers occasional feelings of micromanagement. At the same time, the fact that CA/WW is in on the field of battle, getting dirty along with everyone else, boosts the morale of the team. Everyone is in it together.

CA/WW is the *leader*. It's personal. Everybody feels connected to the leader. The CEO probably hired most of the team personally, knows what they are all working on, and gives them direct feedback when necessary. The CEO is a signal generator who leads by direct example. Everybody on the team knows the CEO—and everybody knows what he or she wants. If the team needs to buckle down for a key product deliverable or customer meeting, the CEO is in the office with them. When stress levels rise, the CEO keeps tempers in check. When there is a victory, the CEO leads the celebration. The CEO and the platoon feel like a single cohesive unit.

2] Captain America and the Avengers: Working through others

Then the CEO job changes. The next CEO job is to hire and lead the Avengers, a band of highly capable superhero-executives who stand shoulder-to-shoulder, ready to do battle against the competition, find GTM-Fit, and accelerate the startup to category leadership. Each part of the company is now run by a superhero—a Sales superhero, a Product superhero, a Marketing superhero, an Engineering superhero, a Customer Success superhero, and so on. Because of their superpowers and focus, they can all do their jobs better than the CEO can do them. The CEO is no longer the jack-of-all-trades hero. The CEO is now part of powerful team of superheroes, and that profoundly changes the job. Now the CEO must work through others. Everybody in the company at this new stage of the journey reports to the superheroes, not the CEO. This is a big change for the CEO and for the team.

Let go, but maintain accountability and visibility. The CEO must now unlearn the heroic do-it-yourself behaviors and instead learn how to delegate, relinquish control, and let go. This shift—from do-it-all CA/WW to the leader of the Avengers—is one of the main failure spots for early CEOs, who are often so full of adrenaline and passion that they fail to recognize when it's time for or the need to change. Or they do recognize the need, but they fail to change due to a fear of losing control, or fear that no one can do the job as well as they can. As a result, the CEO struggles to hire talented superhero executives who see the CEO's inability to relinquish control. The company and the CEO suffer.

> **Bob:** *"Early on, I was heavily involved in product decisions. As we grew, my team got on my case—rightfully so—and demanded that I back off. Sometimes with much stronger words. They were right. We had hired product leaders. I was slowing them down and impacting their ability to drive the product agenda. I had to let them do their jobs."*

Relinquishing control has real risks. Relinquishing control to an underperforming executive can cause major damage to a company. Control is swapped for accountability to goals and some level of visibility, so the CEO must have a way to hold a leader accountable. The CEO must also have enough visibility to sense if a leader is struggling or off track before damaging the company. How can the CEO relinquish control while maintaining control? That sounds contradictory.

"Eye contact" enables a CEO to let go

Instead of managing every task as Captain America/Wonder Woman, the CEO now empowers each superhero to do their job and lead their own team. The CEO must relinquish control to the superheroes, letting them make decisions to run as fast as they can. Letting go requires a level of trust which is fundamental to any CEO-executive relationship. It's critical to enabling Grade-A superhero executives to thrive. In fact, Grade-A superhero executives will not work for a CEO who shows an inability to let go.

The key to letting go, while ensuring execution, is "eye contact" between the CEO and new executive. "Eye contact" is a common view of goals, metrics, resources, dependencies, and culture for which the new executive and their team are accountable. After an onboarding period for a new executive to work side-by-side with the CEO (i.e., two-in-a-box), this kind of eye contact allows a CEO to let go with confidence and the new leader to take the reins on execution.

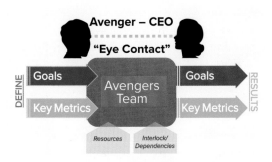

Figure 2: Conceptual model for "eye contact" between CEO and new executive.

What does eye contact look like? The CEO works with the Avengers to define goals and key metrics, as well as the resources and the interlock/dependencies required to achieve them. The output is the results that the Avenger, the CEO, and the board care about.

In this model, the CEO treats each Avenger's team as a "black box," letting the leader execute, using eye contact with the Avenger to keep track of what goes in and what comes out.

In reality, it's not actually so black-and-white. It's more of a dark-gray box: one that allows the Avenger a zone of autonomy yet also provides some level of transparency and acknowledges dependencies with other leaders.

Eye contact: A two-page template

Every CEO should develop a one-or-two-page template that defines what "eye contact" with an Avenger will mean. For example:

Page 1: High level themes, goals, and key top-level metrics.

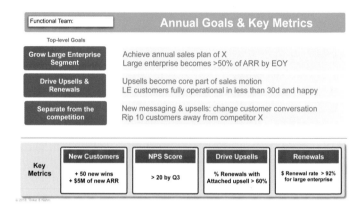

Page 2: Detailed Goals/Metrics and Interlock/Dependencies

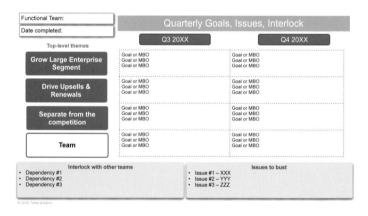

Break out the themes into quarterly goals and metrics that get very specific. And, very importantly, clearly define dependencies (a.k.a. "interlocks") between other teams or the CEO that are required for the executive to achieve their goals. The template can be customized. In this case, this template also calls out top-level issues that need attention to be successful and treats them at the same importance as a goal.

With eye contact, the CEO pulls back from the hands-on CA/WW and lets go. Now, rather than driving every decision, the CEO only gets directly involved in details at times of big decisions, sticky tradeoffs, or major execution issues. The key is developing a sense of when to get involved and when not to. How to know? Identify the right metrics. Pay attention to dependencies. Listen to your intuition. Listen to your superheroes; they will tell you.

Hiring top talent is uncomfortable for everyone. Adding new superheroes to the executive team is often uncomfortable for CEOs. Why? Because superheroes often can—and should—do their jobs better than the CEO. This can threaten less-experienced CEOs. It is easy to say, "I won't be that CEO" who feels threatened—until you're the one who's being asked uncomfortable questions by a sharp new executive. Hiring a new superhero is also uncomfortable for the rest of the leadership team. When a new superhero joins the leadership team, the existing team must adjust. Egos inevitably get bruised.

The classic example of adjustment for the CEO and team is when the CEO hires the first "Grade-A" VP of Sales. Adding a Grade-A VP of Sales to the leadership team is critical to company growth, but it can make a CEO and others profoundly uncomfortable. The VP will push everyone in the company—the CEO, the product team, the marketing team—to the next level. The VP will point out that early customer-acquisition processes that were the pride of the company were actually one-off, unrepeatable sales, and will demand that the company develop a repeatable sales playbook. The VP will force the CEO to realize that product marketing and company marketing need a major revamp. Every resource investment decision will rightly become a tradeoff between adding sales capacity and engineering capacity. Old ways of making decisions and doing business will have to change. Discomfort is normal. Embrace it.

Cement the team of Avengers. The CEO's job is to cement a band of superhero Avengers into a team. How can a CEO tell when the team of superhero Avengers is coalescing around the mission and working together effectively? There are subtle but powerful indicators to look for.

1. **Do they bring in talent?** When individual superheroes put their reputations on the line to recruit talent into their platoon, that's a sign they've bought into the mission.

2. **Do they make sacrifices and tradeoffs with each other?** When individual superheroes are willing to sacrifice their team's interests for the success of another superhero, that's a great sign. It's music to a CEO's ears to hear a go-getter executive say, "I'll give up that resource—it's more important to go over there." When superheroes put the goals of the company and other leaders ahead of their own, they are coalescing as a leadership team.

Ego is the enemy of leadership. One of the biggest mistakes a CEO can make in the transition from Captain America to the Avengers: Let their ego get in the way.

Ego is the enemy of leadership for the CEO and the rest of the leadership team. While some CEOs and superhero executives will inevitably have egos, they will need to set them aside. Great ideas, great execution, and candid feedback should come from everywhere, even if it's uncomfortable for the CEO or for other leaders. With ego, it becomes about the person, not the mission. Success is about the mission.

3] Professor X and the X-men: Enabling an army of superheroes

Now the CEO job changes again. It's no longer enough to lead a band of superheroes, Avengers-style. The company has accelerated to category leadership and must make the leap to become a sustainable industry leader. At this stage, the CEO must preside over and lead an entire army.

This is a very different CEO job. The CEO role becomes more like Professor X in the X-Men, who was the dean of a special university. (It's no coincidence that the X-Men are headquartered in a school.) Each of the superhero executives is now both a warrior on the battlefield and a teacher ringing up the next generation of superhero leaders. Professor X is focused on winning the war rather than any individual battle. Professor X finds himself or herself doing fewer things, but for a lot more people---and repeating themselves a lot.

Do less for more. To scale successfully in Thrival mode, the CEO must do fewer things—but for many more people. The CEO is rarely involved in individual product decisions, people decisions, or customer decisions. Instead, the CEO now has to focus relentlessly on providing vision, driving the company toward its top-level goals, ensuring the right leaders are in the right roles and aligning the teams. Professor X has to always be asking, "Does this topic impact the entire company?" If so, deal with it now. If not, delegate. The CEO must let go of many things that previously felt very important to them and reconceptualize their jobs and themselves. This is an oddly unnerving, but necessary, thing to do.

Focus on the war not individual battles. The Professor X CEO doesn't focus on individual battles; Professor X does whatever it takes to achieve the mission and win the war. Instead of being on the battlefield, Professor X spends more time in the war room, focusing on the kinds of things that win wars:

- **Sharpen and communicate the mission:** This mission must be clear and well-communicated both inside and outside of the company. The team and the market understand where the company is going and why.

- **Be the face of the organization:** Category leaders and market leaders matter in the market. The external market— and internal team—want to see and relate to the leader.

- **Drive execution by setting goals and using metrics:** Setting a few clear top-level goals across the company, on both annual and quarterly time horizon, is crucial to execution at scale. Use quantifiable and time-bound operational metrics to measure results, make decisions, detect issues, and reward performance.

- **Prioritize resources:** Allocating resource pools aligned with goals, strategy, and business constraints is an increasingly important component of the job.

- **Lead change:** What gets a startup from A to B often holds the company back getting from B to C, and then again from C to D. The CEO must lead the rewiring of the company for each new stage.

- **Resolve thorny issues and big decisions:** Big decisions at this stage can largely determine the future of the company. Tradeoffs are not always clear. The buck stops with the CEO.

- **Culture and leadership:** Lead and evolve company culture and company's leadership team to match the needs of the company. Culture is the one communication-and-execution tool that doesn't dull as the company scales. As a matter of fact, it's the opposite: culture becomes an even more powerful and impactful tool for the CEO as the company grows.

The late-stage CEO job is totally different

Ben Horowitz, Partner – Andressen-Horowitz,
Former CEO – Opsware

The job of the early-stage CEO is to get the company to product-market fit, and then to accelerate. Everything is about survival. As Opsware grew, I felt the CEO job change in fundamental ways:

- **Metrics and Instrumentation:** Metrics and instrumentation of the business go from ad-hoc to precise

- **System View:** Instead of looking at functional teams as silos, I had to take the system view, to understand how the different parts of the company, the customers, the investors, and the market were interacting with one another.

- **Teamwork:** Executive evaluation shifted. Instead of evaluating specific skills and an ability to hire, evaluation became more about how well a leader works with their peers.

Perhaps one of the biggest challenges is that the CEO is really the only one who sees how all the pieces fit together—both internally and externally. It's not that a CEO is particularly smart or observant; it's simply a byproduct of the view from the CEO role and the regular interaction across all the aspects of the business. I would sometimes take for granted that others could see the system view and context as I could as CEO. I would jump to conclusions and not share enough of the context and thinking with the team. As CEO, you have to remember that the 360-degree view is unique to you and invest the time to help others see as much of it as you can.

Reconceptualize yourself—or step aside. The leap from the Avengers CEO to the Professor X CEO is particularly challenging. Not every CEO can make this shift. It's a very different job, and requires very different behavior, mindset, and focus.

Often the most difficult challenge for the CEO at this stage is personal. The CEO must unlearn how they *perceive themselves adding value* as a CEO and leader in a startup. The new CEO job often requires disengaging from the very things that, up until this point, were closely tied to how the CEO perceives he or she contributed to the company. Every CEO has a very personal assessment of how they add value every day—it's a key part of the "emotional return on investment" for the insane commitment it takes to be a startup CEO. But what happens when the CEO must deliberately stop doing something that underpins how they see themselves adding value and having earned their role as CEO? The answer is *insecurity*. It creates an intensely insecure "emperor has no clothes" moment for the CEO. The CEO is consciously or subconsciously wrestling with identity and adding value. *When I stop doing the things that I know added value in the past, how will I add value in the future? What is my value to the company? Will people see me as a political leader "just sitting around"?* For a period, the change feels oddly detached. But that is totally normal and exactly what needs to happen.

Successfully navigating the shift requires the CEO to fundamentally reconceptualize the CEO job and adapt themselves as a person.

Some CEOs can make the transition—but some can't, or prefer not to. That's totally okay and represents an important opportunity for the CEO and the board to have an honest conversation about the future.

New CEO role impacts others. The drastic change in the CEO role has a secondary effect on some executives. Some executives will perform better with the new CEO role—the leader thrives on more open space. But some executives' performance will be worse—and those leaders need more guidance. The significant change in the CEO role trickles through the entire leadership team. It is easy for the CEO to miss this secondary impact on other leaders, as the CEO is consumed with their own drastic role change.

Help the Avengers transcend. At this stage in the life of an enterprise startup, everyone is unlearning together. Unsurprisingly, the Avenger executives are now going through their own transformation in parallel, unlearning and facing their own fears and insecurities. The Avengers must go through the same unlearning, rewiring, and letting-go challenges that the CEO faced in the last phase of the startup's growth. The CEO's ability to share the lessons and battle scars of personal transition as a leader is immensely valuable coaching for Avenger executives, improving their chance of success and the company's success. The cycle then repeats itself again and again at every step change in the company.

CEO unlearning moments

Unlearning is painful, stressful, and often messy. Ask any CEO about their unlearning moments, and an awkward or sheepish look will flash across their face as they replay the memories in their head and then begin to share.

Unlearning my fear of short-term turbulence

Bob Tinker, co-founder and former CEO, MobileIron

My biggest mistake: During the fast-growth Thrival stage, I let my fear of self-inflicted, short-term turbulence get in the way of making a hard change to get to the right long-term outcome. As a result, I let important changes take too long.

I spent too much time trying to avoid turbulence. It hurt the company.

I had to unlearn that fear. During earlier Survival stages, self-inflicted turbulence at the wrong time can kill the company. I was wired to loath it. In the later Thrival stage, self-inflicted turbulence might suck for 90 to 120 days, but it won't kill a company. And it's often critical to get to the right long-term outcome.

What are the things that feel like painful short-term turbulence but are often critical to long-term success? A product change that in the near term will upset customers but will be the right thing 9 to 12 months out. A leadership change that creates execution turmoil and team departures but is the right thing for next phase of the company. A major change in market strategy or sales focus that will distract the team and confuse the market for the next quarter but will drive growth 6, 9, or 12 months out.

These things all suck. Investors, customers, and your team will be all over you in the middle of it. Team and investor confidence will wobble. A huge amount of the CEO's and team's energy will be wasted on collateral damage. Hard-fought momentum will taper, giving a competitor extra oxygen. It's painful—but absolutely necessary.

How did I unlearn my fear? I found two things helpful:

1. Building an "alarm bell" into my thinking that rings when I notice myself resisting a big change due to potential turbulence and collateral damage ("Ah, this is my fear of self-inflicted turbulence speaking"). Hearing that bell allows me to remind myself to just push through it.

2. Variable zoom (a concept discussed later in this chapter), which gives you the context—and the courage—to endure disruptive turbulence. Head straight into it, embrace it, and take the heat. The turbulence will pass, and you'll get to the other side.

Unlearning moments: Money, informality, and selling

Phil Fernandez, founder and former CEO, Marketo

As a product-centric founding CEO, I had three rapid-fire unlearning moments that all happened at the same time, as we shifted from survival to growth.

Money: Frugality is crucial to survival. So "Save, save, save" has to be the mindset. But as we grew, I had to unlearn it and instead learn the "Put money to work" mindset—even with unclear ROI. It felt reckless, yet it paid for itself and unlocked growth and scale.

Informality: Marketo and I prided ourselves on informality. As we scaled, informality flat-out failed us. We needed a formalized plan, formalized accountability, and a formalized progress-review process. Healthy growth depends on some level of structure. I came late to this realization.

Selling: Early on, I was a classic product CEO, deep in the customer-product interaction. I would occasionally dive into source code or tune a product capability to meet customer needs. Later, when the company needed my time and energy focused on selling and building GTM, I had to unlearn my tendency to spend time on product and dive into code. I struggled with it. The team went as far as to revoke my source-code access to force my attention to selling and GTM.

Unlearning moment: Evaluating leadership for the future

Mark Templeton, former CEO, Citrix

Building an enterprise startup to over $500M/year was a Herculean accomplishment. Our Citrix leadership team had made the impossible happen. We could not have done it without them, and I was grateful. But now it was time to gear up for the future, by transforming ourselves from a $500M category leader to a $1B industry leader.

I subscribed to the common wisdom: judge a leader's capability based upon results. But results are only backward looking. I had to shift my mindset to evaluate leaders based upon suitability for the future.

I replaced leaders who had contributed mightily, but who I decided were not suitable for what the company needed next. The changes were painful, but absolutely the right thing to do.

How did I unlearn my common wisdom? I found a metaphor from Roman mythology helpful: the god Janus had two faces, one looking backward, the other looking forward. I had to also look in two directions at once to remind myself to differentiate between results and suitability for the future.

Figure 3: Janus, the God of Beginnings, looking both forward and backward

Unlearning moment: Run towards the pain and darkness (even in good times)

Ben Horowitz, partner – Andressen-Horowitz, former CEO – Opsware

In the early days of a startup, the CEO must maintain a tough balance between optimism and being 100 percent clinical about reality. Optimism is what keeps you and the team going. Being clinical about reality is what makes you and the early team able to adjust and find success. It's particularly hard to tell the difference between a growing pain and an existential threat; almost everything seems like an existential threat.

However, as a startup begins to accelerate and show signs of success, the reverse happens. It becomes harder to see real issues. It can be easy to explain away challenges, sweeping them under the rug as a temporary blip on an upward trajectory. Or to make some convenient excuse to let the team and the company of the hook.

One of my many unlearnings was to not accept excuses and let the company, a team, or myself off the hook—even when things were going well. You must maintain the same ruthless sense of reality from the early stage. As a matter of fact, it's more than that: you have to run towards the darkness and pain, regardless of how you feel. During the go-go growth times, it's in the darkness and pain where real issues lurk. The CEO's job is to run towards the darkness and pain and face it head on.

The soul of the startup CEO

Startup CEO is a fascinating job. A lot has been written about the skills of a good startup CEO: vision, leadership, communication, execution.

Equally important, but less discussed, is the "Soul of the CEO"—the internal wiring and behavior patterns that make for a good startup CEO:

Self-awareness, which enables learning and un-learning.

Schizophrenic mindset, which allows simultaneous optimism and pessimism.

Integrity, which serves as the foundation for leadership and culture.

Passion for the mission, which fuels the CEO and the team in good times and bad.

Self-awareness: Looking in the mirror and acting on what you see

A good CEO *must* be self-aware.

This trait supersedes everything else. Self-awareness is crucial to adaptability, learning, and unlearning. Self-aware leaders regularly look in the mirror, evaluating their performance, acknowledging their shortcomings, and diagnosing their bugs—-and acting on what they see. Being self-aware is easy in theory. But being self-aware is hard to do in practice. Self-awareness is deeply uncomfortable and even painful—yet incredibly powerful.

Self-awareness requires changing the way you think and act. It requires recognizing that what made you successful probably isn't what will keep you successful. It means recognizing that one's own behaviors are holding the company back and need to change. It enables profound learning and unlearning.

Self-awareness takes courage. It means admitting mistakes and shortcomings, often publicly. It means evaluating one's own performance and potential and doing what's best for the mission and the company. It can even mean recognizing that one is no longer the right leader for the company.

Most of all, self-awareness requires making yourself vulnerable. Vulnerability, somewhat counterintuitively, builds your credibility and the confidence of those around you. Self-awareness and vulnerability provide a foundation for candor, which builds credibility with the team. Self-awareness and vulnerability underlie the ability to change and evolve on the inside, which in turn inspires confidence from the team. Why? A good team will see a self-aware CEO as one who can learn and unlearn as the company evolves, leading the company through the inevitable challenges and changes on the way to the promised land of success.

Self-awareness can be practiced and developed. The trick for CEOs is to embed it into the daily mental routine. Small everyday situations and large company-impacting situations are all opportunities to reinforce self-awareness. It takes practice, reflection, and a willingness to embrace discomfort head on. Discomfort is normal—a sign that you're on the right track.

3 ways to practice self-awareness

The Mirror Test: Be willing look in the mirror. When you make mistakes, look at yourself and say, "I didn't handle that well. Why not? How do I change to get better?"

The Defense Test: Ask for critical feedback. When you hear things you don't like or that make you uncomfortable, ask yourself, "Was I defensive? Or did I take it and digest it?"

The Vulnerability Test: Admit mistakes publicly and privately. Acknowledge your ignorance, make yourself vulnerable, open up about your insecurities. Talk about your attempts to improve your skills and behaviors.

Those around the CEO—trusted leaders, employees, board members—provide a key feedback loop for self-awareness. A self-aware CEO regularly asks the people around them for feedback and perspective. In some ways, the team knows the CEO better than the CEO knows themselves.

> **Bob:** *"I would regularly ask my team for critical feedback. At first, they held back, thinking it was superficial. It took some time for them to believe that I genuinely wanted to know what they thought, would not get defensive about it, and would take it to heart. But once they realized that I was serious—boy, did they unload on me. Those conversations were often painful and uncomfortable, but hugely valuable. They created a new level of candor and trust. I thank my team for giving me the tough feedback they did. They deserve lots of credit for helping me to evolve and grow as a CEO."*

An outside CEO coach can also play a powerful role in helping a CEO to develop self-awareness and act upon it.

> **Bob:** *"A great executive coach does more than 360-degree surveys and weekly calls. A great executive*

coach crawls inside your head, pushing you to reflect on your behaviors, reactions, assumptions. They help you see reflexes, biases, and assumptions that you don't see, or don't want to see. They—almost like an investigative journalist asking pointed questions—get beyond the 'what' of the situation, and into the 'why.' I had a great executive coach who played a major role in my transition from the Avengers-CEO role to Professor-X-CEO role, which was a particularly tough transition for me. It was messy and painful, but eventually transformative for me and how I led the company."

Self-awareness doesn't mean being a slave to other people's opinions. It simply means paying attention to yourself and doing something about what you see. It may feel like weakness, yet the exact opposite is true. Self-awareness is an oddly powerful thing. It creates the feedback loop that enables learning. It builds trust. It is the antidote to being hardwired—and the key to a CEO's ability to unlearn their way to company success.

Schizophrenic mindset: Confident optimism and total paranoia

Only slightly after self-awareness comes the next most important CEO trait: schizophrenic mindset.

Schizophrenia? Seems counterintuitive, but it's true. CEOs must be optimistic and passionate, inspiring the team and themselves. At the same time, they have to be completely paranoid, constantly looking over their shoulder, worrying about everything that can go wrong. They have to inhabit both mental states at the same time.

The dualism is constant and critical for the company's success. On the outside, a CEO is always aggressively recruiting, raising capital from investors, speaking at conferences, and closing customers. On the inside, the CEO paranoidly focuses on everything that could go wrong, is deeply attuned to where all the wobbly parts of the company are, and lies awake at night worrying about the fast-closing competitor. The CEO must project confidence and belief to lead the company along the path to the promised land, inspiring hope for the employees and the board through dark times. At the same time, the CEO must clinically assess the current reality and risks in order to make the right decisions.

There is a danger to this dualism. When the gap between these two personas becomes too large, it strains credibility. The trick is to strike a balance, projecting the right image at the right time, and in the right measure. It is difficult to maintain this duality. There is no hard and fast rule for this. It's the reality of the job. Don't worry when equilibrium is occasionally lost; it happens.

Being both self-aware and schizophrenic can be emotionally and mentally exhausting for a CEO. The constant introspection and duality required for the job make it a very lonely one—but they also create a powerful opportunity for personal and professional growth.

Integrity

Integrity is the foundation for credibility and trust in the CEO, which in turn is the foundation for leadership and the company culture. Integrity of the CEO impacts everyone related to the startup: executives, employees, customers, board, and shareholders. Operating with integrity is a must for the CEO. Losing integrity damages the company and can trigger a death spiral. Integrity does not always mean knowing the right answer, but it does mean that those around the CEO believe he or she is always acting honestly and forthrightly.

Passion for the mission

Passion for the mission is the nuclear reactor inside the CEO. It creates the energy that fuels the CEO and the team. Passion— for the product, for the customers, for the team, for the company itself—attracts great talent. It inspires customers to buy. It inspires investors to invest. It carries the CEO and the team through the inevitable tough times—when sales results fall short, when product deliverables are late, when a big competitor takes the company on, when optimism is in short supply, and when even stalwart supporters begin to have doubts. In those times, passion is what carries a CEO—and a company—to the other side.

CEO skills for decision-making

A core of the CEO job is to make decisions. CEOs are inundated with decision requests from employees to executives to board members. When there is ample data, making decisions is easier. But startup CEOs operate in highly dynamic environments with limited time and limited information to make a decision. Below are three skills that help the startup CEO make decisions.

DECISIONS AHEAD

Develop a "sixth sense" for the business

Early on, because of the day-to-day with customers, product, and people, the startup CEO develops an intuition about the business. The CEO can sense the company almost like a living organism with inputs, outputs, muscles, bones, antibodies, and emotions that can help predict where things are about to go awry.

> **Bob:** *"Potentially bad situations tend to have a sort of shimmering distortion field around them that signal strain or trouble. It's difficult to put a finger on what it is. It's some combination of interconnected signals, people avoiding the topic, a gap in visibility, and, well, some bad vibes. Regardless...when something feels weird, it probably is. Push through the shimmer. Dig into the situation and find the reality."*

As the company grows, the CEO must let go of many details, and the hard part becomes how to maintain a sixth sense that can still detect those shimmers while letting go of the details. Simply looking at summary metrics will cause the sixth sense to atrophy and eventually blind the CEO's intuition. The key is to have a feel for what's underneath the summary metrics. A good way to do this is to pick three or four "scope points" that offer the CEO visibility into the details of the business. The point is not the details themselves; rather, it's that they offer the CEO the ability to detect patterns, notice problems early, and maintain an intuitive feel for the business.

> **Bob:** *"Even as the company grew, in order to keep a feel for how things are going, I did something that my executives thought was nuts. I insisted that I stay copied in on three things: the sales win/loss reports, every new*

employee offer letter being sent out, and the customer-service escalation report. I didn't police them, and I didn't even look at them every day. I'd periodically scan the win/loss reports for patterns or new information, check out the new hires see who was being hired into which team, and pick out customer escalations and read the notes. The exact data didn't matter. It gave me a direct view to what's happening on the ground, both good and bad, and helped maintain my sixth sense for the business."

Variable zoom: Micro, macro, and everything in between

The myth is that successful CEOs just focus on the big picture. That's total baloney for the enterprise-startup CEO, who constantly must zoom in and out—from the big picture out on the horizon, tactical details right in front of their face, and everything in-between. CEOs must constantly adjust their focus like a variable-zoom camera lens.

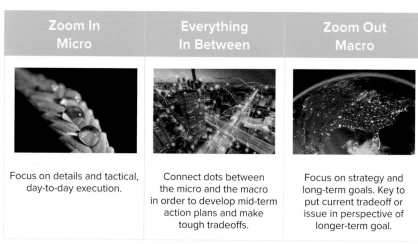

Zoom In Micro	Everything In Between	Zoom Out Macro
Focus on details and tactical, day-to-day execution.	Connect dots between the micro and the macro in order to develop mid-term action plans and make tough tradeoffs.	Focus on strategy and long-term goals. Key to put current tradeoff or issue in perspective of longer-term goal.

An analogy for "variable zoom" is how a baseball outfielder intuitively process information in order to catch a fly ball. When a batter hits a ball, the outfielder instantly processes the macro view: How hard was the ball hit? Where's it likely to go? Which way to move? Then, as the ball travels through the air, the outfielder instinctively makes an in-between plan to catch the ball—running towards it, eyes following the ball, adjusting speed, direction, hands, and feet to all be in the right place at the right time. Finally, the outfielder's eyes bring everything down to the micro view—glove placement, timing, and closing the mitt around the ball for a successful catch. Variable zoom in action.

Variable zoom for a CEO is similar. It's like a mental algorithm that's always running, allowing the CEO to process every situation with a mix of short-, medium-, and long-term perspectives. Successful CEOs use variable zoom to both take in the big picture and focus on the details, all while being able to connect the dots in the critical middle ground that informs the goals, action plans, and decisions that drive a startup's month-to-month and quarter-to-quarter execution towards the endgame. Without variable zoom, CEOs and other leaders might be able to tell you what the ideal world looks like in three years, or they might be able to drill into technical details of the here-and-now, but they can't successfully navigate and connect the dots in the critical middle ground of action plans, decisions, and sequencing that transforms the here-and-now to the endgame.

Sequencing matters: What to do, in what order

A key part of the CEO job, it's often said, is deciding what to do and what not do to. That's true, but it's an oversimplification, and it mistakenly leaves out an equally important aspect of the enterprise startup CEO job: sequencing. Early-stage startups operate with limited resources, so deciding what to do in what order is just as important as deciding what to do and what not do. Sequencing manifests itself in a number of thorny "catch-22" dilemmas often faced by startup CEOs:

- **Customers vs. Capital:** A startup needs customers to raise capital, but a startup can win customers without a product—which requires capital.

- **Good vs. Good-enough-for-now:** A startup engineering team is constantly asking what needs the extra effort to be build rock-solid now ("Good") vs. what just needs to be Good-enough, where a team could circle back and fix it later. This is a sequencing catch-22. Overbuilding part of the company too early is a misallocation of precious time and, in the case when that part was not needed, it is a waste of precious resources.

- **Team vs. Capital:** A great startup needs to hire a great team; a great team wants to join a company that is well-funded; and investors want a great team before investing. Another catch-22.

It's the CEO's job to figure out a way through these sequencing dilemmas.

Common mistake: Sequencing is a linear batch process

Some first-time startup executives, particularly those who come from larger companies, attempt to build their startup in an efficient, logical, and structured manner. That logical manner sequences the main actions—raising capital, hiring a team, building a product, and winning customers—as a linear batch process of step 1, step 2, step 3, and step 4.

Figure 4: Startups do NOT work like this; they are not a linear batch process.

Much to their surprise, the startup never gets going. Why? Building a startup is not a linear batch process. The catch-22 sequencing dilemmas make a linear approach nearly impossible.

Proper sequencing is more like an upward spiral

Proper sequencing can solve this problem. Visualize the building of a startup as an upward accelerating spiral of minor (not major) milestones that are sequenced and inter-related. Each milestone is small enough to execute upon successfully, which then signals enough progress to justify the next sequence of milestones.

The startup spiral of sequenced milestones is not a batch process, it is more like a continuously flowing chemical manufacturing process that has to be in balance. Under-doing one area creates a bottleneck, which holds the whole process back. Overdoing things in another area can waste precious resources. Each stage feeds the next, iterating in a loop that helps accelerate the overall process.

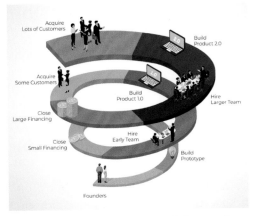

Figure 5: The Startup Spiral: Sequencing small milestones unlocks progress

An example for the enterprise startup: Increased lead-generation feeds more sales headcount, which then requires more sales investment, which then drives more wins, which increases pressure on support, which then impacts customers add-on expand orders for the next year. Simultaneously investing across the board is both impractical and wastes extra capacity before it's needed. The same goes for engineering and product delivery. CEOs spend a lot of their time and energy figuring out how to sequence limited resources and milestones to keep the process (a.k.a. the company) accelerating upward. As every new milestone is achieved, that part of the company accelerates, which feels great. Yet, that acceleration immediately creates a new bottleneck somewhere else that holds back the company's growth. The CEO and leadership team will feel like they are constantly chasing the next bottleneck around the company. That's natural, and it is also a useful model for how to think about how and what to sequence. The good news is that every solved bottleneck removes the next constraint and helps accelerate the startup to success.

CEO skills for execution

Not only must a startup CEO make decisions, a startup CEO must also communicate, get people on board, and drive execution in order to win.

Distillation and repetition

Early-stage CEOs are involved in everything. They simultaneously communicate and execute on many different things, get them done, move on, and then never look back.

A later-stage CEO's communication patterns and execution focus are different. It's counterintuitive, but as the company grows and increases in complexity, CEO execution and communications must simplify. A CEO's execution focus is on fewer, more important goals. The CEO's communication is distilled to a smaller number of simple points.

Pay attention to the CEOs of large successful startups. They speak in a very limited number of carefully prepared sentences. They distill their focus on a small number of top goals, and they repeat those key points over and over again.

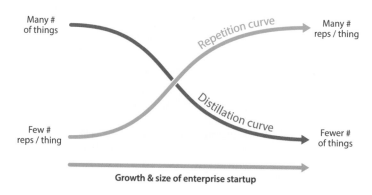

Figure 6: Distillation and Repetition Curve

To the CEO, this increased distillation feels lame and insultingly simplistic at first. In fact, the exact opposite is true. CEOs who carefully distill their communication to simple points come across more powerfully to the company. As the company scales, the larger pool of listeners is more likely to remember and act on several simple powerful points. This distillation does not come naturally to many first-time CEOs; it takes practice.

Repetition is equally powerful. Repetition of several key points ensures that the company understands and acts on the CEO's message. Early-stage CEOs are frequently frustrated by regular repetition because they've succeeded by making points, setting goals, and moving on. But as a startup grows and succeeds, the CEO must become a repetitive signal generator to ensure the Avengers and the rest of the army are aligned and executing on the mission.

Increased distillation and repetition are particularly acute in the transition to the Professor X role.

> **Bob:** *"Distillation wasn't natural for me. As the company scaled, I had to work on it, by boiling my main points down to one, two, or three things. Distillation became increasingly important for everyone to get the same simple and powerful message.*
>
> *The repetition part drove me crazy at first. I felt oddly insecure. I kept wondering if I sounded like a broken record and was being tuned out by the team and customers. But then I realized that constantly reinforcing the same message was exactly what we needed to execute at scale."*

Get people on board: The ability to close

Everybody says that CEOs have to be good at selling. That's true, but it misses a much bigger point: CEOs need to be good at closing.

Closing goes way beyond selling. The ability to close is a pervasive ability to get a diverse set of people—customers, investors, employees—to converge, commit, and join you on the enterprise startup journey. Closing a big enterprise customer. Closing a major-channel sales partner. Closing a new round of funding. Closing a key new executive hire. Closing the management team on the goals for the next 12 months. Closing the entire company on the need to make a major directional change. Closing is one of the most fundamental jobs of the startup CEO.

> **Bob:** *"A good enterprise-startup CEO is always closing. Closing customers. Closing channels. Closing leadership hires. Closing investors. At first, these things all seem different. As a first-time CEO, it took me a while to figure out that all those situations are actually related. Closing is a horizontal skill that cuts across the CEO job. Convincing others to commit and jump on the startup bus with you is a fundamental part of the startup CEO job."*

The good news: Closing is a skill that can be learned and practiced. Some people have natural skills, but most learn it over time. There are plenty of non-salesy technical CEOs who had no idea how to close at the beginning of their startup journey but managed to figure it out and build an enterprise startup into a great company.

Push outside comfort zone: Think in swim lanes

In the very early stages of an enterprise startup, searching for Product-Market Fit often means the CEO is absorbed with building the product. Or perhaps the first-time CEO comes from sales or marketing and naturally gravitates to their comfort zone—spending time with customers. This is natural. Yet, very quickly, the enterprise startup needs the CEO to be the leader for *all* aspects of the business. The CEO must think and spend time differently. The CEO must break out of the comfort zone and unlearn skills and lessons that worked in the past, in order to do a more holistic job. But how? By thinking in "swim lanes."

> **Bob:** *"I struggled with this transition. Inertia led me to spend 80 percent of my time on product and customers, iterating and trying to win. That's where my comfort zone was. But the team needed me to be working on the overall company and, very importantly, charting the execution path forward for the team. A CEO coach pushed me*

to adopt a new mindset: Think in swim lanes. It was a powerful tool that snapped my mindset to be a more holistic CEO and help chart the path for the company.

I drafted my swim lane plan in pencil on an 11 by 14 sheet of paper. That drawing became the map for what we needed to do, how I spent my time, how things were linked, and how we measured progress. It was a living document that evolved with the company. It hung on the wall of my office, eraser marks and all. I still have it."

The swim lane model

To create a swim lane plan, do three things:

1. Define the swim lanes: What are the major swim lanes for the whole company? Examples could be: Product/ Engineering, GTM Sales and Marketing, Customers & Customer Success, Team & Culture, Financials & Fundraising (or whatever make sense for your team).

2. Set the target and work backwards. Establish a medium-term target for each swim lane, which could be 6, 12, 18 or 24 months out (again whatever timeframe makes sense for your team). And then work backwards from there, setting key interim milestones that indicate success.

3. Nail down dependencies. Link milestones and interdependencies across the swim lanes.

Suggestion: To make clear how goals and progress relate to raising capital, add a line (and update it over time) for when the startup runs out of cash (ZCD = Zero Cash Date).

Step 1: Define swim lanes for the whole company

Draw a set of the of the major swim lanes for company execution.

Add a line for the company's zero-cash date. Move the date as the company's financial situation changes.

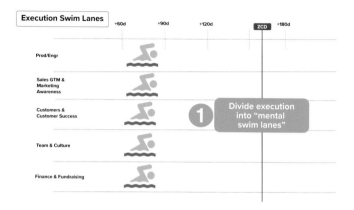

Step 2: Establish a medium-term target for each swim lane and work back from there

On the farthest right column, write down the key long-term outcomes the company is aiming for.

Now work backward to identify the key interim milestones that will tell you are on track. This is harder than it sounds, particularly when you've been living in iteration mode of just putting one foot in front of the other.

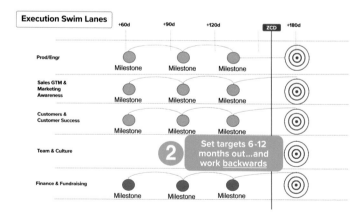

Step 3: Link milestone dependencies across different swim lanes

This is the time to think about dependencies. What milestones in one lane depend on milestones in other swim lanes? Does a sales target require a key product capability? Does achieving a product goal require a key resource to be on board by a certain time? Is a delayed milestone in one area impacting another?

Since this is a living, breathing document, feel free to do it with paper and pencil. Beauty is not the goal; utility is.

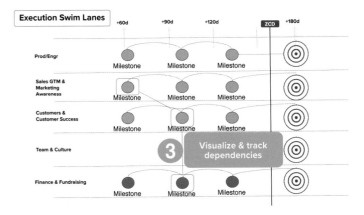

The swim lane model helps CEOs move out of their comfort-zone and develop a holistic mindset. It maps out an execution plan that moves beyond one-foot-in-front-of-the-other iterative execution. It provides the team with a powerful communication tool. It reveals where the CEO spends time, rightly or wrongly. It provides an early warning system for where a company is off track. It allows the CEO to become what the company needs: a leader who sees across the company, thinks ahead while working backward, and who leads the rest of the team to do the same.

Advice for first-time CEOs

The CEO is a huge signal generator

Every move a CEO makes is not only watched but is also interpreted for meaning. This makes the CEO a huge signal generator. This signal generation is a force that can be used for good, for bad, and even by accident.

Examples of CEO signal generation

- **For good:** Confident body language in important meetings will spread confidence in the business and the product.

- **For bad:** Multitasking and answering texts during an executive business review will convey a lack of belief and interest in the project, or confidence in the presenter.

- **By accident:** Stomping grumpily into the office after getting pulled over for speeding on the way into the office, the CEO inadvertently triggers worry across the team that something bad happened to the company.

Even what a CEO pays attention to is itself a signal. CEO attention is like a flashlight, signaling an interest in the things it shines on. By simply paying attention to something, on purpose or by accident, a CEO sends a signal that can cause a team to prioritize something or change their behavior. It's like the Heisenberg's Uncertainty Principle: simply observing the state of matter changes its state.

Offhand CEO comments become accidental commands where teams run off and follow the CEO's wishes, disrupting existing goals and plans, frustrating everyone. An off-the-cuff comment in a meeting two weeks ago gets replayed out of context and gradually becomes dogma.

Everyone is watching the CEO. All the time. This creates an additional level of responsibility and self-monitoring and self-awareness for CEOs. They need to be careful and deliberate in their actions and communications, but there is a fine balance because they must also remain authentic. Don't let the self-monitoring create paralysis.

Simply be mindful of the effects that words and actions have on the team. There's no simple way to manage this. Just do your best. Stay cool. Stay positive. And be yourself.

Be both ruthless and sensitive

CEOs have to make tough and sometimes ruthless decisions. Decisions that are the right decision for the business can often hurt people. Employees who worked hard for the company sometimes get fired; their lives are affected. They have to go home to their spouse with their head hung low. A sales rep worked for a year to win a big deal, only to have the product slip and the deal canceled, sees their sales commission paycheck cut in half. A team of engineers worked for a year on a new product initiative, only to have the project canceled due to a need to cut expenses. Customers who made a bet on the company get hung out to dry when a key product capability is canceled; their career can be damaged. These situations all stink.

While the CEO must make ruthless decisions, showing sensitivity to the impact of the decision goes a long way with those impacted and the people around them. Sometimes sensitivity means explaining the situation candidly. Sometimes it means making a special exception to demonstrate loyalty. Sometimes it means simply listening and showing empathy. The best CEOs are ruthless when it comes to making decisions but are still sensitive to the very real impact that these decisions have on people. Running a growing startup demands both ruthlessness and sensitivity.

> *Tae Hea: "My thinking on the CEO decision-making process has evolved. As a young investor, I clinically considered the strategy and financial implications of a decision and stopped there. Now I encourage CEOs to consider the delivery and implication for team and culture as well.*
>
> *As an example, a portfolio CEO asked for advice on a situation with a newly hired VP of Sales. The new VP Sales had spent significant effort on a big deal and was on the verge of beating their first quarter's sales targets, but the big deal required major product customization.*

The big deal was great. The major customization was a problem. Did the customization add value to other accounts? No. Would the product customization crowd out other needed development projects? Yes. The strategic decision was clear: Don't do the big deal. Five years ago, my advice would have been the simple, ruthless answer: Tell the new VP Sales 'No' and move on. But since then my perspective has changed. The new VP Sales was enthusiastically doing exactly the job they were hired to do: Close deals. And, a CEO's first several months with a new VP Sales is a critical time to build trust. So, my advice has changed over time: I still suggested that the answer had to be 'No,' because that really was the right business decision. But I also recommended that the board relieve some sales quota pressure from the VP Sales, which demonstrated sensitivity to the importance of a new CEO-VP Sales relationship. That way, the CEO could say 'No' but still demonstrate support for and trust in the VP Sales."

Build a web of trust between leaders

A CEO must build trust with their leadership team. Equally important is for the CEO to help the members of the leadership team develop a web of trust *among themselves*. In the early days of a startup, building trust between leaders is simpler because every leader can easily see what the other leaders are doing, which naturally builds trust. As a startup gets larger, building trust between leaders gets harder, since the leaders have less visibility into the goals and day-to-day operations of the other teams. With less visibility, trust between leaders develops more slowly.

Phil Fernandez, the founding CEO of Marketo, describes the challenge of building trust as the difference between rowing one big boat and rowing a bunch of smaller boats. Early on, all of the leaders and the CEO are in one boat, rowing as hard as they can. Every leader

Figure 7: Single boat vs. a flotilla of boats

can easily see and understand one another's interdependencies and execution, which builds a common understanding and trust. After rapid growth, though, the company feels more like six boats rowing in parallel, each with a leader in the front of the boat. The leaders at the front of each smaller boat don't understand the mission of the other boats and can't see their day-to-day actions. Lack of understanding and lack of visibility between the teams in the different boats slows the building of trust and undermines confidence.

CEOs must be able to build trust across the different boats and help each boat understand the missions of the other boats. CEOs must foster transparency and regular interaction between the leaders of the boats. With trust between the leaders, the flotilla of individual boats will act together, fighting as a single large warship.

"1:1 eye contact" leads to "Many:Many eye contact"

As discussed earlier in this chapter, the eye contact between a CEO and an Avenger leader is fundamental to build trust between the CEO and the Avenger. Establishing eye contact with each Avenger leader has a fascinating and productive side-effect of creating Many:Many eye contact among the Avengers, thus helping build and reinforce a web of trust among the leaders.

Each "eye contact" between the CEO and the Avenger establishes the goals, metrics, resources and dependencies—which is exactly the type of visibility that peer executives need to understand from each other. Providing visibility into each other's "eye contact" helps drive execution among the Avenger leaders. And at a personal level, understanding and visibility provides the foundation for web of trust between the leaders.

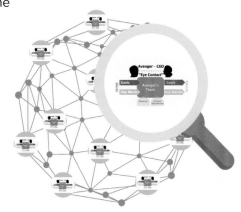

Crystalizing "systems view" of the company

Aggregating these eye-contacts helps the CEO understand the business. It crystalizes a systems view of the company. For the CEO, being able to visualize how all the different parts of the business (each led by an Avenger) fit and work together to drive execution is critical to leading the company, and in many ways, can help simplify some complexity out of the CEO's job.

Aggregating the views

By lining up the key aspects of each Avenger's eye contact document the CEO can then see how goals, metrics, resources, and dependencies line up and fit together into a systems view and tie to the overall company goals.

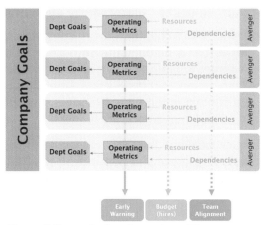

Figure 8: Conceptual systems view of the company

As discussed earlier, the CEO still lets each Avenger run their team as a black box, while negotiating the Avengers' output (departmental goals) and input (resources and dependencies from other avengers) and having the right operating metrics to see if the Avenger is on track.

This frees the CEO to focus on the system level. Are the Avengers' goals tied to the overall company goals? Are the key operating metrics on track or are there early warning signs? What is the aggregate resource and expense commitments and how does that fit into the budget? Is the company on track for hiring? Are the key dependencies between the teams being managed effectively? Is the team aligned and making tradeoffs?

The CEO needs to ensure that the department goals lead to the company goals, that the sum of all the resource requirements drives headcount and operating expenses, and that the dependencies are being met by the other Avengers.

Sample "systems view"

This is an example systems view showing the go-to-market (GTM), customer success, and finance teams.

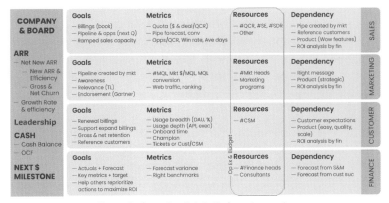

Figure 9: Sample of detailed systems view

Relate to sales teams

To a product-centric (or any non-sales centric) CEO, sales teams can feel alien and mercenary. But an effective and motivated sales team is key to winning customers, finding GTM-Fit, and accelerating the business. To relate with sales and get the most out of the team, a CEO has to develop two key traits: empathy and motivation.

> **Empathy.** CEOs often don't appreciate how tough it can be to work in sales. It's hard to try to sell but get rejected over and over. It's hard to have 50 percent of your paycheck be uncertain, depending wholly on your ability to win customers and achieve sales targets—all while being dependent on product, marketing, and customer-service functions outside your control. Meanwhile, those non-sales functions are impatient with sales as to why potential customers are not buying: "It must be a sales-execution problem. Our product is great. If only they understood how to sell it." The salespeople are out advocating and taking personal financial risk, while at the same time

being squeezed between the internal execution reality and potential customers who want everything now. CEOs need to show their sales teams that they understand the sales job and want to help sales succeed.

Motivation. To motivate their sales teams, CEOs need to understand what makes them tick. Understand what drives them to fiercely go out and sell, and what causes them to stall. Understand their intrinsic motivations and financial motivations. Understand how sales territories are set and compensation plans work. Understand how to align each sales person's motivations with the company's goals. Understand the short-term and long-term tradeoffs that salespeople must deal with every day. Understand their motivation and relate to it. All this can even become fun for the CEO.

Sales teams are critical to the success of the enterprise startup, and usually the largest expense. Sales is a system that is a mix of people, emotions, and process. Understand them, relate to them, motivate them, invest in them, and they can become a fearsome GTM machine.

CEO tough stuff
Damned if you do, damned if you don't

CEOs experience tons of no-win situations. Sometimes there is no good choice. Sometimes by fixing one thing, the CEO knowingly makes another situation worse. Sometimes by solving a critical issue now, there will be painful payback later. Sometimes, depending on who you talk to, the CEO is either too early or too late, too harsh or too nice. It's the reality. CEOs just have get used to it.

One early startup rang a "deal bell" whenever a sale was made. It was fun and a celebration. The startup then accelerated, closing dozens of deals per day. Eventually, the bell ringing started to feel routine, with some employees complaining it was distracting and unnecessary. So the CEO decided to stop ringing it. In a sort of Pavlovian irony, this troubled some naturally skeptical employees outside of sales, who felt that eliminating the bell rings meant that the company was winning fewer deals and trying to hide the bad news. Damned if you do, damned if you don't.

There are all kinds of common scenarios:

CEO situation	Damned if you do	Damned if you don't
Making changes to key people	Changing out an important leader creates short-term turbulence, gaps in execution, and attrition.	Not making the change creates long-term execution and team problems.
Celebrating achievements	Ringing the "deal bell" with every customer win becomes routine, and employees tune it out.	Not ringing the "deal bell" fails to recognize achievements, and the team worries about business progress.
Deciding when to fire someone	Moving quickly suggests you didn't give them a chance, negates a culture of learning, and creates a fear of making mistakes.	Moving slowly suggests you are not decisive enough and tolerate poor performance.
Deciding how quickly to grow the financial operating plan	Cranking up the plan for high growth creates excitement, higher expectations, execution capacity, and improved valuation, but also increases risk levels of execution failure.	Establishing a modest growth plan sets lower expectations, which can be met, but leads to lower sales and lower valuation—a potentially worse outcome than execution failure.
Deciding which deals to win and which to lose	Winning every deal is aggressive and drives up sales in the near term, but often jacks up expenses and spreads company resources too thin.	Deciding to lose deals can be strategically prudent, but a competitor publicizes your loss, damaging your reputation and other deals, and the internal team perceives a lack of winning attitude.
Deciding when to discuss a potential big change	Previewing changes with people helps the team feel included and heard. However, as the future changes leak out, politics escalate, distractions and fears increase, and the CEO looks disorganized.	Not previewing change with the broader team avoids creating distractions and fears but generates feelings of exclusion.
Briefing prior to board meetings	Frequent communications and briefings ahead of board meetings helps make them run smoothly but absorbs significant CEO time—often when the board itself wants the CEO to spend more time growing the company.	Infrequent communications and no briefings save time but make for more-volatile and less-focused meetings. CEO is perceived as not proactively seeking input and listening.

Damned if you do, damned if you don't. It stinks. But it's a reality of the job, so be ready for it. Take comfort in knowing that every CEO struggles with them. Try to strike the right balance for you and do what you think is right.

The internal-momentum trap

Startups experiment with several paths, figure out which one gets traction, and then run down that path as hard and fast as they can. The CEO embraces the successful path with passion and provides positive reinforcement. As the company races down its path, it wins customers and gathers momentum. Everybody feels as though they're on a single grand mission.

Then a big change is needed—maybe in product direction—to focus on a better growth opportunity, or in GTM execution, to focus on a better sales model, or adjust to a change in the competitive landscape. Now, ironically, the agile, fast-moving startup struggles to make the change. What's going on? It's caught in the internal-momentum trap.

The longer a startup moves in a certain direction—by pursuing a particular GTM or product strategy—the harder it is for the team to change course. At one level, this is purely mechanical: it's hard to stop or turn sharply if you're racing ahead at breakneck speed. But it's also psychological: changing course can feel like a betrayal of mission to a startup team, or at least like a diversion of focus. CEOs therefore have to strike a tough balance between being faithful to the path ("We just have to keep hammering") and being practical ("Just because we're on this path now doesn't mean that we always have to be"). Breaking out of the internal-momentum trap is painful, and it sometimes creates collateral damage. In the extreme case, some early employees, feeling betrayed or disillusioned, may leave the company. That's totally normal: those who don't buy into the change *should* move on. Make the call, accept the turbulence, and move on. The CEO's job is to drive the business.

The emotional roller coaster

Everybody in a company, especially the CEO, will go through huge emotional swings in the early stages of a company, sometimes in the blink of an eye.

Tae Hea: *"When I was the early CEO at Airespace, I once went from the highest of highs to the lowest of lows in five minutes. After a great meeting with a potential OEM partner, I felt a rush of optimism and hope about our future. Then I walked out of the conference room and bumped into one of our key engineers—who submitted his resignation. I was on the CEO emotional roller coaster."*

During the crazy highs, remember things are never as good as they seem. During the crazy lows, remember that things are never as bad as they seem. Zoom out from the week-to-week ups and downs, and stay focused on the destination.

Under assault and all alone

The startup CEO job is lonely. People say this so often that it's become a cliché. But it's true, and there's more to it than meets the eye. As CEO, you're all alone *and* you're under assault from all directions. Every major business issue and business request lands on your desk. Every major people issue and people request does too. Everyone always wants something from you, and there's never enough time or resources to satisfy everybody.

In the dark moments of a startup, the CEO is surrounded by people but is in many ways alone. The CEO is accountable upward to the board and downward to the leaders and the team. The CEO must serve the customers and react to market and competitive forces. CEO is stuck alone in the nexus of the company, getting hit from every direction.

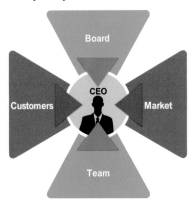

Figure 10: The CEO: Surrounded by many, but also alone

The good news is that CEOs often have more support available to them than they realize. Board members, team members, and customers all care about the welfare of the CEO. Everyone looks to the CEO for leadership, looks to the CEO for results, and looks to the CEO for inspiration—and is committed to help. The CEO is far from alone. Ask for help, and be amazed how many pitch in.

CEO execution cadence

Ultimately, it comes down to execution. The CEO's execution cadence drives everything—and it evolves as a startup grows. What is the CEO mindset? How does the CEO set goals? What are the top priorities? How do the CEO and leadership team drive execution week-to-week and month-to-month? How does the CEO communicate with the company? Every CEO develops their own execution cadence. Be explicit about what you want it to be—and be conscious of how it needs to change as the company changes. There are no precise rules for this, but here are some suggestions.

Evolution of CEO execution		
Captain America/ Wonder Woman and Platoon	Captain America and the Avengers	Professor X and the X-Men
Mission		
Don't Die!	**Win the Battle!**	**Win the War!**
Set Plans		
Thesis about problem and opportunity	Annual company goals and formal rollout	3-year company goals
Set three key milestones (e.g., product, customers, funding) and devise a short-term battle plan to hit milestones	Quarterly goals by leader	Leadership goals cascade into sub-team goals
	Clear interlock and dependencies	Budgets and metrics target allow for decentralized planning
Execution Cadence		
Executives run a scrum model: twice-weekly executive stand-ups	Quarterly leadership off-sites	Regular cross-functional business reviews
Lots of hand-to-hand combat	Weekly executive team meetings for 3-5 hours to cover both operations and big-focus topics	Create extended leadership team beyond top executives
Everything else dealt with ad-hoc	CEO holds regular company all-hands discussions	CEO broadcast: regular reinforcement of vision and top-level goals

Startup CEO: The best, the worst, the profound

Being a startup CEO is great job...most of the time. It's chaotic and stimulating, yet also lonely and exhausting. Being a startup CEO is an opportunity to make a difference by building a company from the ground up that matters in a market, creates value in the world, and positively affects the lives and careers of your team. The job catalyzes unmatched professional and personal growth. The startup CEO journey is a crazy, steep learning curve and a profound exercise in self-awareness that transforms the CEO as a leader and as a person. Enjoy the ride. Good luck!

PUNCHLINES

» As a company changes, the CEO job changes. So, must the CEO change themselves.

» In the beginning, the CEO job is like Captain America or Wonder Woman. Then the job changes to be more like Captain America and the Avengers, where each Avenger is an executive with their own superpower. Then, at scale the CEO job is more like Professor X and the X-men, where Professor X is the dean of a university.

» Unlearning is key for the CEO. What gets a CEO from A to B is often what holds the CEO back in getting from B to C. Company success depends the CEO's ability to rewire themselves and reconceptualize themselves and the job. Change or be changed for the good of the mission.

» The "Soul of the CEO" (self-awareness, schizophrenic mindset, integrity, and passion) are just as important as the skills of a CEO.

» CEO skills can be learned and practiced. Some will come naturally. Some will be more difficult.

» Advice for first-time CEOs: Be willing to adapt. Be aware that you are a signal generator. Build trust. Push outside your comfort zone.

» Being a CEO is tough. CEOs are constantly on duty—all alone and under assault from all directions. The role is full of damned-if-you-do, damned-if-you-don't situations. It's an emotional roller coaster.

» Being CEO is great job. It's a chance to build a company to achieve the mission. It's a chance to build a team and a culture that comes alive. It's an energizing professional growth experience. It's a profound personal growth experience. Have fun, and enjoy the ride!

CHAPTER 2:
LEADERS

In Survival mode, everyone, including the founders, is an individual builder and an unofficial leader. There is no room for extras. Leadership is fluid and task-dependent. Early team members bring special skills, and depending on the task at hand, different people are looked to as unofficial leaders at different times. The CEO and early product leaders drive the company, the mission, and the team. Overall, there is very little official people leadership. So-and-so is the leader for back-end platform. So-and-so is the leader for product-user interface. So-and-so is the leader for customer engagement. Everybody on the team has a simple job that they're doing together: survive long enough to find PM-Fit and GTM-Fit in order to unlock growth—before running out of cash.

Survival leaders: Early stars emerge

Survival is a hardship stage. The team is limited. Capital is limited. Everyone's iterating on product and customers. Directions constantly change. The search for PM-Fit and GTM-Fit will make or break the startup. Uncertainty runs rampant. Stress runs high.

The strain of Survival forges early stars. The early stars of an enterprise startup do what needs to be done. They demonstrate leadership in the face of impossible odds.

Early stars are found across the startup. Some stars are new to startup leadership. Some stars are highly experienced over-hires who love early stage startups. The early sales engineer helps to win the first customers, provides critical feedback to product management, tunes product-marketing pitches, and dives into customer support. The early QA leader pulls all-nighters iterating on a new-product release, designs a new network diagnostic tool to help customers, and runs IT as a side job. The early customer support engineer works both US and European hours nearly every day to help early customers. The early engineering leader, listening to a customer's challenge, proceeds to invent an entirely new product capability that eventually becomes a core part of the product architecture.

Building a startup is hard. Every startup is challenged, facing a lack of resources, talent, and customers. It is easy to become negative, like Eeyore in *Winnie the Pooh*, who only sees doom and gloom in every challenge. Eeyore-like negativity sucks the life out of a startup. It's toxic for an enterprise-startup team. Avoid the Eeyores.

Figure 11: Avoid the Eeyores that see doom and gloom (Winnie the Pooh, *Walt Disney*)

Stars embody the "can do" spirit of the early startup. They don't let the lack of resources, talent, or customers demotivate them. Like Dory in Pixar's *Finding Nemo*, they are energized by the opportunity of learning and overcoming challenges. Stars are energized by the opportunity to create something from nothing and face challenges head-on.

Figure 12: Early stars are like Dory, energized by adventure (Finding Nemo, *Pixar Animation Studios, 2003*)

Early stars get amazing things done with very little. They wear multiple hats, delivering Herculean individual efforts. They iterate quickly, often without a grand plan. They are lionized for their outsized contributions, deservedly so. They become the core of the early startup team and the bedrock that defines the company culture. These early stars propel the company through the painful challenges of Survival. They are energized by the opportunity to win customers and prove PM-Fit, the opportunity to figure out a winning GTM playbook and achieve GTM-Fit, and the opportunity to unlock growth—earning the right to be a leader in a fast growing startup.

Thrival leaders: From individual stars to a band of superhero executives

GTM-Fit unlocks growth and marks the transition from Survival ("How do we not die?") to Thrival ("How do we win?"). In Thrival mode, the startup accelerates on the path to become the category leader. In Thrival mode, every leadership job profoundly changes. What was done by an individual star is now done by a team. Individual stars are now asked to build and lead teams. Small tiger teams of five people expand to teams of 50, 100, and 200 people. In some cases, leaders now lead teams that are larger than the whole start-up was a year ago. Being a leader now demands more than individual stars making Herculean individual efforts.

To accelerate, the startup now needs a leadership team of super-hero executives, who have their own special superpower and who can build and lead a team.

- The sales superhero rapidly hires a team and builds an enterprise GTM machine.

- The product and engineering superheroes keep up with rapidly accelerating market requirements while ensuring current enterprise customer needs are met.

- The customer success superhero builds an engine that can ensure success for a rapidly growing company with a brand-new product and a global customer base.

- The marketing superhero rapidly accelerates sales-lead generation to support the GTM machine—while building awareness and brand that will help the company become a category leader.

Each superhero must lay down a blueprint of growth, rapidly attract and hire a team of high performers, and deliver.

Shifting gears to accelerate from Survival to Thrival is both a blast and super challenging for the startup leaders. Mindsets change. Execution changes. Planning changes. Culture changes. Leadership roles change. *Everything* changes, and every leader must adapt in order for the company to make it through the crazy game-changing acceleration stage to category leadership—and beyond.

Then scale: Superheroes to super-leaders

The superhero journey is never done. Superheroes spearheading their teams through the crazy changes of acceleration to category leadership is a proud accomplishment. But once that's done, the leadership jobs change—again. Superheroes must now transcend to become super-leaders—the leaders of leaders who direct large teams and complex operations around the world and, in turn, hire their own band of superheroes. The calculated recklessness of rapid growth gives way to the operational fortitude, planning, and predictability required by a category-leading company operating across the globe. Intensely focused "tribal" leadership gives way to a style that puts more emphasis on effective cross-functional leadership. The key to all of these leadership changes—unsurprisingly—is *unlearning*.

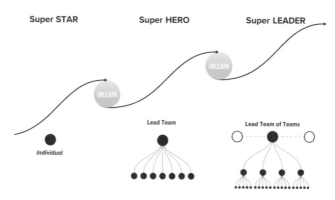

Figure 13: Superstar to superhero to super-leader

The superhero leader must unlearn many of the leadership behaviors that made them successful in the acceleration stage and must now transcend to become the right super-leader for the company's next stage. Sound familiar? It should. The superhero executives must now evolve—just like the CEO evolved from Captain America/Wonder Woman and the Platoon to Captain America and the Avengers. Just as that evolution was bumpy for the CEO, the evolution is a bumpy for the executives, and many don't succeed. But when it does happen, seeing superhero become a super-leader is a wondrous thing to behold.

Superheroes and super-leaders: Are they hired or made?

For the sake of the mission and the startup, success in the Thrival phase requires that the leadership team becomes first a band of superheroes and then transcends to become a band of super-leaders. This raises a profound question about stars and early superhero leaders, and the job of answering it rests squarely on the shoulders of the CEO: Give the early star a chance to become a superhero? Give the superhero a chance to become a super-leader? Or avoid the risk of failure, and instead hire a new leader who is proven at the next stage?

Some superheroes and super-leaders are *made*. They are highly adaptable and gifted stars who transcend their original role to become a superhero, or even super-leader. They inspire others to do the same. They become part of the fabric of the startup's success story. Transcending is a huge morale boost because it reinforces a culture of learning and professional growth. It creates the recruiting brand. The startup becomes known for developing great talent, which attracts even more great talent—a virtuous circle.

However, many superheroes and super-leaders are *hired* because hiring a proven executive was the right answer for the company and shareholders. That solution is really hard on the early stars. It makes them feel that the CEO doesn't have confidence in them and doesn't appreciate their commitment and sacrifice. They feel unfairly capped. At that point, some stars quietly fade away. Others become bitter, negative cultural forces and get fired. Some adapt, maturely identifying the opportunity to learn from the startup's growth and an experienced superhero, so they can transcend in their next startup leadership role.

The decisions are some of the trickiest decisions for a CEO. Each decision on a leader impacts the company's success and sends a strong cultural message. Each decision also comes with a very important audience—the rest of the company. (More on this later in the chapter.)

How do leaders transcend?

Making the transition from one leader role to the next is one of the biggest professional growth challenges there is. Some leaders are naturals and make it look easy. But for most leaders, transition is stressful and turbulent. A large portion of leaders fail on their first try.

While painful in the moment for everyone, do the right thing for the startup and learn from the failure. Leaders who desire to learn and adapt will internalize lessons from their failures and use them when they try again. They may or may not succeed, but simply attempting the leap to the next leadership role is a powerful learning and personal-growth experience for every leader. Embrace it.

Three steps to leadership transcendence:

- **Recognition:** The leadership role is changing.

- **Unlearn the old role:** Let go of what made you successful.

- **Anticipate and embrace next role:** Expect discomfort.

Recognize leadership role is changing

Role changes often sneak up on startup leaders. Their titles, compensation, and reporting haven't changed, but as the startup grows, the leader's role fundamentally changes.

> *Frank Marshall, former VP Engineering at Cisco, and a board member of Aerohive Networks, Covad, Juniper Networks, MobileIron, and NetScreen: "I do think the biggest issue with the changing roles [transitions between levels] is that you really don't know they are happening. And then you wake up and the damage has been done."*

The CEO role changes again and again as a startup moves from Survival to Thrival—and other leadership roles do the same. Although the VP Sales title is the same whether the company has just one sales rep searching for PM-Fit, or ten sales reps in acceleration, or 100 sales reps in category leadership, the job itself differs dramatically at each stage. The same holds true for VP Engineering and CFO, and every other leader.

Unlearn the old role: Let go of what made you successful

As leadership roles change, people must change themselves to adapt. Leaders must unlearn their old job, rewire behaviors that have now become reflexive, and learn the new leadership role, all while continuing to execute, day in, day out. For the leader and the company, this unlearning requires rewiring oneself in the midst of a high-pressure startup situation. The leader must continue to deliver on sales, product, marketing, and support the best way he or she knows how. As we shared in the book introduction, the unlearning feels like flying in a plane that's desperately trying to gain altitude while re-wiring the plane. It is painful and scary for any leader, yet it's absolutely necessary.

What makes change possible is a *desire and willingness* to unlearn and relearn. No one can force this. It has to come from the inside. Everyone will say they want to change, but, deep down, do they really want to? Some superheroes don't. They are so good at what they do that they want to keep doing it rather than learn new skills and grow. Nothing wrong with that. They are great at their jobs and want to keep doing them. But other leaders embrace the challenge and opportunity that comes with the painfully hard work of unlearning and transcending as a leader.

Even for those leaders who embrace change, it's not easy. Do they recognize that the skills that helped them succeed in their current job are becoming liabilities for their next job? Are they willing to re-wire nearly instinctual behaviors? Can they transform how they communicate with their team? Can they radically change how they use their time? Can they become a different type of leader? To get to "yes" on these transcending questions requires self-awareness and a desire to change at a very personal level.

Anticipate and embrace the new role

To make the leadership transcendence even more difficult, startup leaders rarely have a clear view of what the next leadership role looks like. Some leaders are fortunate to have a mentor or CEO who can clearly articulate the requirements of the next leadership role. Most startup teams have not been through the journey before, so most are left to figure out what that next leadership role looks like without a clear picture of what's ahead. This visibility gap unnecessarily increases the difficulty for startup leaders—which leads us to the next section.

Demystifying the next startup leadership role: GTM, Technical, Finance

Fortunately, there are patterns of how leadership roles change as the startup changes. The patterns are not exhaustive and don't apply to every enterprise startup, but the themes will be similar enough to help CEOs, boards, and, most importantly, the leaders themselves to anticipate and adapt.

As a startup moves from Survival to Thrival, its leadership roles have three profound transitions: survival, growth, and scale. In each transition, the leadership role changes drastically; many of the skills and behaviors that made the leaders successful now get in the way. Each transition is full of unlearning moments and turbulence.

Below are summaries of the leadership role changes that take place for the GTM leader, the technical leader, and the finance leader on their journey from Survival to Thrival. For each

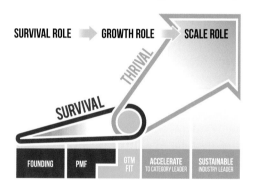

role, we outline each, describe how it morphs over time, and share unlearning anecdotes from enterprise startup leaders who have been through the pain.

GTM leader: Role change & unlearning moments

In the earliest stages of a startup, the sales leader is often one of the founders—finding early prospects, convincing a customer to try a prototype, landing the first couple of live trials, or even the first paying deals. Product-centric founders have a unique ability to sell, which is a strength but also a weakness. Founder-led selling is rarely repeatable.

Startups must bring in early GTM leadership—even if their sales motion is more automated and marketing-led. Early GTM leaders are usually not a big-time VP Sales. Instead, early GTM leaders operate more like **the 18th-century frontiersman Davey Crockett**, who had to find the "path through the woods" that others could then follow. The early Davey Crockett GTM leaders iterate and experiment with different pathways to repeatability and GTM-Fit. (See Book 1, Chapter 3, GTM-Fit).

When a startup achieves GTM-Fit, the role of GTM leader evolves drastically. Now the role is to accelerate the little startup to category leadership, beating out small and large competitors. This role resembles **Joan of Arc** or **William Wallace (a.k.a. Braveheart)**, who built, led, and inspired a warrior army against the much larger enemies in battle after battle. The Joan of Arc/Braveheart GTM leader perfects the GTM Playbook battle plan, hires other warriors, and executes the playbook over and over again to drive growth, beat the competition, and accelerate to category leadership.

At scale, the startup is no longer a startup. It's a fast-growing enterprise category leader with a complex GTM machine; it runs operations around the world and often has multiple product lines. The GTM leader at this stage resembles **General Eisenhower**, the commander of Allied troops during WW2, who was not a dashing battlefield leader or master battlefield tactician but rather an architect who led from the war room, an organizer of disparate groups, and an operational mastermind. He could harmonize diverse groups and disparate personalities into a smoothly functioning coalition. The scale GTM leader must architect, build, lead, and operationalize a large and increasingly complex GTM machine that simultaneously delivers predictably and takes the company from category leadership to industry leadership. The scale GTM leader has to let go of the battlefield behaviors and personal relationships that create the trust, personal *esprit de corps*, and define the very essence of the Joan of Arc/Braveheart leader, and instead change from battlefield commander to the general-of-generals in the war room.

	Early Leader (PM-Fit/GTM-Fit)	Growth GTM Leader (Accelerate to Category Leadership)	Scale GTM Leader (Sustainable Industry Leadership)
	**Davey Crockett**	**Joan of Arc/Braveheart**	**General Eisenhower** (front, center)
Mission	Find a path through the woods: PM-Fit and GTM-Fit. Find and win early customers.	Build and lead sales team into battle after battle against a larger enemy. Drive growth and acceleration from the battlefield.	Architect, build, lead, and operationalize the GTM machine to win the war. Be the general-of-generals in the war room.
Hard Skills	Build the GTM Playbook. Self-sufficient across sales, product marketing, and lead generation. Basic forecasting and GTM metrics. No Sales Ops.	Execute the GTM Playbook. Sales-planning decisions driven by pipeline and growth. Not so focused on efficiency. Sales Ops 1.0: forecasting and compensation. Recruit like-minded warriors and trusted GTM team from past companies.	Architect and instrument GTM machine to provide predictable growth and sales efficiency. Expand beyond single GTM playbook. Contend with increased complexity and agendas. Sales Ops 2.0: machinery for planning, decision-making and long-term forecasting. Hire sales generals and battlefield commanders accountable for top- and bottom-line numbers.
Soft Skills	Find customer hotspots and adjacencies. Work closely with product team.	Establish strong GTM culture and *esprit de corps*. Articulate needs back to rest of company. Pushes team, sometimes uncomfortably. "Win the battle" reputation for competitiveness.	Business-first and operationally minded. Leadership that transcends personal relationships and trust. "Win the war" mentality that balances near-term and long-term, often requires painful sacrifices.

Unlearning moment: From the battlefield to the war room

Mark Smith, four-time SVP Sales – Rubrick, Arista Networks, InfoBlox, and NetScreen

The most difficult leadership transition for me as VP Sales is stepping off the battlefield and into the war room. Being on the battlefield during the acceleration stage— closing customer deals, jumping on airplanes, beating the competition—is a blast. I love telling customer war stories at company all-hands, mentoring loyal brothers and sisters in arms, and running through walls to hit sales goals. It's how I and other VP Sales define ourselves and our contribution to the team.

What I've learned, though, is that at scale, those are the wrong things for a sales leader to do. Driving success at scale required me to change how I spent my time—and completely redefine how I *personally* added value each day as a sales leader. Those changes created an odd sense of insecurity in me and painful shifts in important personal relationships.

Orchestrating our army from the war room meant less time for me in the field, and fewer battlefield stories. Architecting the sales machine and operations is a less personal leadership role that distanced me from sales reps and deals on the ground. Making strategic investment and organizational decisions for the good of the company sometimes personally hurt battlefield comrades who trusted me. Ensuring the right leaders were in the right places meant less time for mentoring up-and-coming junior sales reps. This all hit my self-perception of value, my relationships, and my ego, yet they were the exact right thing to do for the company.

Ironically, GTM leaders face a powerful headwind when shifting from the battlefield to the war room: **a loss of respect**. In each one of my last three sales leadership roles, as I shifted from leading on the battlefield to orchestrating at scale in the war room, I felt a waning of respect from many of my early sales warriors. The temptation was to preserve that respect, dive out into the field, and spend lots of personal one-one time together, but that wasn't what the company needed from me as a sales leader. Making the transition to scale sales leader meant changing how I perceived myself and how others perceived me—for better or for worse. I had to unlearn my old job and let go.

The World War II movie *Twelve O'Clock High*, starring Gregory Peck, captures the dynamic of a leader having to change themselves as their job changes. Peck's character is a squadron commander who is then promoted over time to general. By the end of the movie, he has changed, and his relationship with his early team changed—the evolution was painful and awkward. He feels his former squadron lose respect as he is no longer a battlefield leader. I have all my leaders watch the movie, and then we talk about it. That movie never gets old for me.

Technical leader: Role change & unlearning moments

While finding PM-Fit and GTM-Fit, the technical leader is maniacally focused on developing a product quickly to please the customer—constantly iterating, adapting, and sometimes failing. That means close interactions with teaching customers. Meanwhile, the technical leader has limited resources and limited time. This first role resembles a **frontier craftsman** creatively building a cabin with no blueprint to work from and only the surrounding raw materials and a few neighbors to work with—before winter arrives (when the company runs out of cash).

Once the startup finds GTM-Fit, the technical leader has significantly more resources but dramatically higher expectations. The technical leader during acceleration is under immense pressure—delivering exciting new category-leading capabilities to win new customers, buttressing the existing product to satisfy existing customers, all while out-executing the competition. The craftsman role now becomes a **general contractor during a chaotic construction boom**, who is executing by adding new rooms, while simultaneously remodeling existing rooms and building out a team of subcontractors. Focus shifts to timely delivery, quality, architecture, rapid hiring, resource allocation, and dealing with tradeoffs between competing projects.

Then, at scale, the technical leader job changes again from building a single product to a larger platform, often involving multiple products. Each product has the same challenges as the prior stage—getting the right resources, meeting the delivery and cost targets, and having the right leader—except now the products are linked together into a broader platform. This technical leader role resembles a **real estate developer building a campus of buildings** over multiple years. The office buildings are each separate projects, but they all fit together with roads, open space, and shared infrastructure like parking and utilities. The technical leader must decide when to give latitude to sub-team product leaders, and when to enforce commonality. When to prioritize "individual building" needs over "campus" objectives. Where to invest now, and where to prune? Like the real estate developer, the technical leader at scale balances business decisions, architecture decisions, and execution decisions across simultaneous projects, and is accountable for financial returns and cost targets. Making decisions about investment, execution, and resources across a large set of technical projects at different stages requires operational processes and machinery. And maintaining a technical culture across teams with hundreds of employees scattered across the globe requires a new level of leadership and communications.

	Early VP Engineering *(PMF/GTMF)*	**Growth VP Engineering** *(Category Leader)*	**Scale VP Engineering** *(Industry Leader)*
		 Source: UCSF History Page *One of first buildings in the redeveloped San Francisco Mission Bay*	Source: SF Office of Community Investment & Infrastructure *Redevelopment plan for San Francisco Mission Bay*
	Frontier craftsman	***General contractor***	***Campus developer***
Mission	Build product 1.0 with rapid hands-on iteration and limited resources to find PM-Fit and GTM-Fit.	Build category leading product while out-executing the competition.	Build out platform and multiple products, delivering on vision and business results.
Skills	Customer obsession. Hands-on coder or system architect Rapid innovation and mastery of new technologies. Lead small team, hired mostly through trusted network.	Step back from hands-on coding to drive overall engineering execution. Balance between exciting category-leading capabilities and buttressing product for current customers. Build and lead multiple engineering teams. Hire strong bench of first-line leaders. Recruit beyond network.	Lead multiple simultaneous engineering programs, all linked to overall strategy. Drive investment decisions, dynamic resource allocation, and execution across products at different stages. Instrument product-delivery machinery to drive planning, resource allocation, measure results, and predict outcomes. Become leader of leaders. Lead global team. Blend hired and acquired talent.
Challenges	Deal with uncertainty and frequent changes. Hire key technical talent into an uncertain startup. Know what can be done quickly (and potentially redone later), and what must be done carefully to ensure the foundation for the right long-term architecture.	Build linkages across customer support, sales, and marketing. Expand core product functionality, while paying down technical debt. *(See Book 1, Chapter 2 on tech debt.)*	Balance needs of individual product teams with needs of overall company. Avoid ossification of execution due to inertia and complexity. Maintain intimacy with all products and technology.

CHANGE OR BE CHANGED

Unlearning moments: Letting Go. Comfort with Gray.

Jason Martin – EVP Engineering FireEye

I had multiple major unlearning moments over the last five years on my way from being the CEO of a 35-person startup to EVP of Engineering, leading a team of over 800 people spread across the globe. Learning is painful; unlearning can be even more painful. Old habits die hard. In particular, the very habits and techniques (often very beneficial habits) that contributed to your success die even harder.

There was no eureka moment. The realization dawned on me slowly, through introspection, discussions with my teams, and frustration that "what used to be so easy" became harder. What worked in the past as a technical leader in the early days of my career no longer worked (or didn't work as effectively) as my teams scaled. The ways I communicated, managed projects, and provided technical oversight in the past were failing. The tighter I held on, the more I was getting in the way and not providing what my teams actually needed from me. The unlearning was painful, but satisfying in retrospect, and I learned a lot about myself.

Unlearning moment 1: Mourning and letting go of who I thought I was

As a technical leader and technical CEO, I prided myself on my subject-matter expertise, technical credibility, and my ability to dive in with my teams and help. These skills played a large role in my career. In my head, I felt that maintaining and demonstrating that expertise is what created respect from the teams I led. They were fundamental to how I viewed myself and my value to the team as a leader.

As my team grew past 200 people, I spread myself thin across multiple teams. I quickly became overwhelmed, becoming less effective by diving into each decision and issue. As I shifted more toward people management, I witnessed the technical skills in which I prided myself and felt the team respected me for begin to atrophy. My team started to chide me with comments like "you're just doing slides and spreadsheets" or "you're not a real engineer anymore—you're management." There was good-natured humor in that jibe, but it hit a real nerve with me, as it likely would with any technical leader. Yet, I was doing exactly what the leader of a 200-person engineering team must do. This further amplified when the team grew to 800 people. I had to realize that it was going to be extremely challenging to stay close enough to the technology and the code to keep up with my best engineers. I went through a real mourning period, when I felt the gradual loss of that expertise and, in my own head, respect. Eventually, I found inspiration in reframing my role from "building things" to "building teams that build things." That was satisfying.

Unlearning moment 2: Getting comfortable with the grays

As a software engineer, I knew there was a right and wrong way to build a code module, a right and wrong way to architect a platform, and a right and wrong way to do unit testing. There was an answer. I love the clarity and pride that comes from building things the right way. As an executive in a now-large software company with multiple products and a team of nearly 800 people, the right answer isn't always clear, and the information needed to make a decision was often far less than perfect. As the operation grew, I was initially frustrated with the gray "fog of war" that comes with a larger operation, craving the clarity and precision of an engineer.

I've found that most challenges in any organization are related to people and people are not binary. I found that streamlining functions in an organization was significantly harder than streamlining code. I had to unlearn the black/white or right/wrong mindset of the engineer, and instead learned to look for the "edges" of a situation to create a picture in the fog and be comfortable with shades of gray. It wasn't natural for me, but I got better at it, and it's now become intellectually stimulating and even fun.

Finance leader: Role change & unlearning moments

In the early days, the finance leader is very much geared toward ensuring startup survival: the job requires developing an operating plan, controlling expenses, watching cash, helping sales close deals, and helping the CEO raise capital. In practice, this means the job often becomes an early-stage CFO or a VP Finance who acts much like the **supply quartermaster** on the field of battle, ensuring the troops have what they need to fight and survive, while also doing everything possible to conserve supplies.

As the company moves into the acceleration phase, the startup needs a growth CFO, whose job is like that of an **airplane navigator**: laying out the plan of where to fly, deciding whether to go faster or slower, using metrics to determine if the flight is on-course or off-course, and hoping the plane doesn't run out of fuel along the way. The growth CFO doesn't just work with the CEO. The growth CFO also works closely with the GTM leaders to instrument the GTM model to decide where to invest and when to speed up or slow down. The growth CFO works with the product teams to make investment decisions. As a result, the CFO, along with the CEO, are the two leaders at this stage who see all the parts of the business.

As the company hits category leadership and starts gearing up for industry leadership, the CFO job changes again. The scale CFO becomes a **copilot** for the CEO, together building market value, driving operational scale, instrumenting the business for predictability, and enabling investment and de-investment decisions that drive shareholder value. Externally, the scale CFO plays a key role with Wall Street and public investors.

	Early CFO/VP Finance (PM-Fit/GTM-Fit)	Growth CFO (Category Leadership)	Scale CFO (Industry Leadership)
	 **Supply Quartermaster**	 **Airplane Navigator**	 **Copilot**
Mission	Tactical planning and cash conservation	Set course and speed. Drive the business plan. Instrument business for growth.	Partner with CEO to run the business and build business value.
Hard Skills	Build operating plan for Survival phase. Control expenses. Develop intimate knowledge of cash burn and zero-cash date. Build the early GTM financial model and key metrics.	Build operating plan for Thrival phase and growth. Plot the course: Build financial plan and analytics to help make investment and growth decisions. Determine speed. Develop key metrics to track GTM, unit economics, and levers to speed or slow growth.	Instrument business for long-term sustainability. Deeply understand business drivers to drive decisions and allocate resources to mainline business and leadership bets. Develop metrics and operational processes throughout organization to measure results, enable scale, and deliver predictability.
Soft Skills	Help with sales deals and customer contracts. Help with fundraising and due diligence.	Help GTM leaders with plans, quotas, forecasting, and productivity models. Develop credibility with investors to secure and deploy growth capital.	Team up with executives and business units to develop plans and allocate resources. Communicate and build credibility with Wall Street and analysts.

Unlearning moments: Not always being right. Relearning my sense of purpose.

Fred Ball, four-time CFO at Marketo, Webroot Software, BigBand Networks, Borland Software

In finance, we invest a lot of time and effort in building a great financial model. We take great pride in that model, since it shows our deep understanding of the business. Having the right model and executing against that right model was how I added value as a finance leader.

As we grew, the natural next step was to apply the financial model rigor to other parts of the business—in particular, to analyze and challenge the other functional leaders with the rigor of a financial model.

Over time, I had to unlearn the desire to always be right (or have the right model). I realized it was more important for me to help the other executives become successful than to be right with the financial model myself. Instead of analyzing from the outside (or illustrating the "rightness" of our model), I had a new mission: help the other executives see how their operating reality tied to the numbers and business model, and whether their operational beliefs were actually validated by the metrics in our plan. In some cases, we would help the leaders illustrate their function's plans and performance to more numerically minded executives and the board, which changed the dynamics of the executive staff and board meetings in a positive way. The scale CFO goes beyond the plan and the model, works to ensure that the leadership team is successful, and helps synchronize the different parts of the business. The scale CFO becomes the CEO's copilot.

This scale CFO role required me to be much more integrated with the executives and their operations. I could no longer be deep in the model that I was so proud of. I had to hire a top-tier VP Finance to shoulder much of the load I had been carrying as CFO. That hire was tough on me emotionally, because it challenged my sense of value and purpose as the CFO. With a top-tier VP of finance, would the company still need me? Would my value wither away? I got anxious and developed a subtle emotional resistance to change.

Then we hired a great VP Finance. At first, this was challenging, as I wanted to stay close to the model and impress the team with my depth of knowledge. But then, gradually, I let the new executive take over many of the "CFO things" that I previously had felt only I could do. While it was scary in the moment, six months later I found that letting go had allowed me to step up in my role, be more outbound-focused, and become the CFO the company and our shareholders needed for the next stage. And in doing all of that, I had recaptured my sense of value and purpose.

Helping leaders transcend to the next role

Transcending requires understanding and anticipating new challenges. It also requires leaders to let go of successful behavior patterns. It's a profoundly uncomfortable growth experience—a deeply personal mixture of learning and unlearning about what it means to be a leader.

How can the company help a leader transcend the current role and adapt to the next?

Learn	*Stretch/Push to think like the next role*
Transparency	*Candid feedback*
Unlearn	*Let go of old role. Use rule of 30% to help*
Get Help	*Mentorship and coaching*

Learn: Stretch/push to think like the next role

Learning the next leadership role is tough and particularly bumpy for existing leaders because it's piled on top of existing responsibilities.

Pushing oneself to shift perspectives and think like the next role takes up already-scarce mental energy. Taking on stretch assignments while executing day-to-day requires mental discipline, and tricky priority balancing, as the stretch assignments will naturally feel less important than existing ones. CEOs can help promising leaders by providing stretch assignments to develop new muscles and challenging leaders to adjust their thinking to the next level. The reality is their leadership job is changing and stretching in real time. The key is for the leader, like an athlete already on the field of play, to "stretch in place."

Stretch in place: Think 12 months ahead & present it

A good way to stretch leaders is periodically ask them to think 12 months ahead. Make them focus on three questions in particular:

1. What will your team's goals be?

2. How will your team be executing?

3. What will your team look like?

But have them do more than think about these questions. Have them present their ideas, perhaps at an annual strategy meeting with the board, or at an executive offsite.

Often leaders are so busy putting one foot in front of the other that they don't have the time or the perspective to imagine how their roles, and the company in general, need to change. That's natural. Forcing leaders, including the CEO, to think ahead and present their ideas, catalyzes a change in perspective that is critical to stretching a leader.

For company execution, these think-ahead discussions are incredibly important. For the board, it is a terrific opportunity for key discussions and feedback. For the other executives, each leader learns by listening to the others. For the executives themselves, these presentations are a profound opportunity to get their head around the next role, stretch themselves to evolve with the needs of the company, and begin to transcend to the next role...or it becomes apparent that they may not be able to.

Be transparent: Candid feedback

The textbook advice is to be transparent, providing candid feedback and coaching. That's the right advice because it needs to be done. Any good leader wants and deserves the candid feedback and transparency. It is absolutely critical that the CEO and leader clearly articulate the needs for the next role at the next stage of the startup—and talk about what's going well and what's not going well. Giving candid feedback and coaching is paramount to any leadership role. Leaders owe it to their team. Thoughtful and candid feedback is both a gift to be given—and a gift to be received.

Being open to take candid feedback and coaching is equally important to giving feedback for *both* the leader and the CEO. The good news: high performers who have a healthy dose of self-awareness and willingness to adapt can transcend to the next role. The bad news: unfortunately, some of the most passionate high performers have an almost religious zeal to their past performance that can limit receptivity to change and feedback. While giving candid evaluation can create some risk, provide it anyway. A leader who cannot receive constructive feedback is less likely to transcend. Receiving and giving direct feedback is the only way we grow.

Encourage unlearning: Let go with the "rule of 30 percent"

As a leader's role changes, the biggest unlearning challenge leaders struggle with is "What not to do anymore?" Letting go is hard. Letting go requires a fundamental change in behavior, and in many cases, a part of the role that engenders pride and self-satisfaction. Fortunately, there's a rule of thumb that can help a leader identify these sticking points and make a clinical decision to let go: the "rule of 30 percent."

Rule of 30%

Whenever a leader finds they spend more than 30 percent of their time on any one function, issue, or organizational topic, stop and ask, "Why?"

The answer often comes in one of four forms, each of which demands a specific response:

Answer	Response
1. Demands have scaled	Hire someone to offload the 30-percent demand
2. Leader is doing stuff they shouldn't	Let go and allow someone on the team to step up
3. Leader is backstopping a team member who is now struggling	Evaluate team member and consider making a personnel change
4. It's a spike (e.g., fundraising) that will pass	Do nothing. It's a passing spike. Things are okay for now.

This rule helps provide a clinical lens to help a leader identify how they are spending their time and where to make a change in behavior.

CEOs can use this rule to change their own behavior and evaluate their executive team, an executive team can use it to evaluate itself, and so on, all the way down the organization.

Get help: Mentorship and coaching

Mentors for executives come in all shapes and sizes, but two kinds are often the most valuable: seasoned and recent. Seasoned mentors are very senior executives, with 15 to 20 years more experience, who are deep reservoirs of wisdom and multiple professional experiences. Recent mentors are younger executives with only three to five years more experience, who have recently wrestled with similar growth challenges. Mentors periodically provide on-call help, advice, and perspective, all of which can be vital in helping an executive through periods of challenge and change.

For near-term career growth and challenges, we recommend mentors who are three to five years ahead of the executive, rather than 15 to 20 years ahead. Recent mentors are often more effective for growing executives, as they have more recently lived through similar challenges, and their advice feels more relatable.

Coaching is a more focused form of help for a growing executive. Some of it must come from the CEO in the form of regular feedback and clear conversations about expectations. However, many leaders, particularly those going through big step changes as a leader, can benefit significantly from an external executive coach—an unbiased third party who can play a transformational role in helping the executive rewire for the next leadership role.

A great coach will both push and pull the executive, forcing a level of self-awareness that comes with significant discomfort. That discomfort is the sign of a good coach and a leader who is embracing the opportunity to grow and change as a leader.

Can the superstar or superhero transcend?

All leaders asks this of themselves. For the CEOs, they want their stars and superheroes to succeed. A superhero's success helps accelerates the company, signals increased opportunities for the team, and builds overall confidence and morale. A superhero's failure damages the company, signals fewer opportunities, and saps team confidence and morale. How can a CEO know if a star can succeed at the next level—*before* running an expensive and dangerous experiment? Asking several specific questions can help.

Does the star recognize the need for change?

Rising to the next level requires a leader to change themselves and how they operate. To do that, the most important factor is that the leader must recognize the need to change themselves and their behavior. That requires self-awareness. For superstars and superheroes who have been great at their job and recognized for that greatness, it is often easier and more comfortable to often believe they can just keep doing what they've been doing. Recognizing the need for change is often uncomfortable for them, as is acting on that need. But both are critical if they are to transcend to the next level.

Can the star overcome insecurity and the fear of hiring new top talent?

For a superhero or superstar, hiring top talent is a critical measure of success. Yet, particularly for first-time leaders, this can raise uncomfortable questions: "What happens if they're better than me?" "Will the new hire take away some of my spotlight?" "Will the new hire be so good at their job I'm not needed anymore?" Insecure leaders who allow themselves to be unsettled by these questions are likely undermine the company and themselves—by hiring only unthreatening, B-grade talent; by hiring great talent too slowly; or by hiring great talent, but then disempowering them until they quit. For leaders to rise to the next level, the question is, "Can they overcome this very natural insecurity, and instead hire top talent, empower them, share the spotlight, and let go?"

Does the star want to run faster or run better?

Phil Fernandez, the founding CEO of Marketo, had a simple question when evaluating or coaching a leader for the next role: Does the star want to run *faster* or run *better*? The test involved asking the star to describe the key goals, challenges, organization, and processes for today—and then for six and 12 months out. How would they increase qualified leads tenfold? How would they handle ten times more customers? How would they cope with an explosion of feature requests? How would they address ten times the amount of support tickets? How would they contend with growing cash burn? How would they deal with *all* of that? Their answers showed how well they understood and could address the exponentially growing demands on their teams.

Stars with a "run faster" mentality tended to respond that their teams will just work faster to meet the growing demands. They often felt like the victims of tough working environments, and their typical plans involved hiring "another me." Their solution was more people doing the same thing.

Stars with "run better" mentality, on the other hand, tended to respond that their teams would work differently to meet the growing demands. They viewed tough working environment as challenging puzzles, and to solve them they tried to devise better strategies, organizations, and execution plans.

Here's a simple visual that helps conceptualize the difference. To address the need to carry an ever-growing load at a faster and faster speed, a Run Faster leader thinks about finding more horses, whereas a Run Better leader thinks about restructuring the team to use trucks.

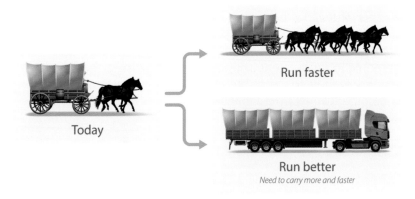

Today

Run faster

Run better
Need to carry more and faster

When leaders don't transcend: Change the people

Sometimes leaders are unable or unwilling to transcend to the next role. In some cases, a fast-growing startup outpaces a leader's ability to adapt and change; in other cases, a leader simply prefers their current role and mode of operating. In both cases, the solution is to change the people.

| Company Δ | → | Role Δ | → | People Δ |

with no Δ in title

...or Δ the people.

Leadership changes are hard. While making the change is the right decision for the startup and the mission, individuals' careers and families are impacted. Making a big leadership change takes resolve and candor, while at the same time compassion and a way of allowing people their dignity. Every change creates turbulence, so be ready for it. Every change also is a terrific opportunity to rewire and make operational changes, so take advantage of it. Every change is also an opportunity to demonstrate leadership and signal to the company and other leaders, so use it wisely. Change is hard, but change is an opportunity. Embrace it for the sake of the mission.

The "superstar/superhero to mere mortal" problem

When a leader was a mis-hire or not performing in their role, the decision to make a change is straightforward. A much more difficult and challenging situation is when a star or superhero who played a major role in building the company fails to unlearn and change as the company's needs change. These honored leaders go from superstars and superheroes to "mere mortals." It's brutal. In fact, it's one of the hardest things for startup teams to wrestle with.

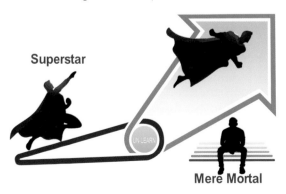

How does it happen? Painfully for the leader and those around them.

The company changes and, for a while, the superstar and superhero continue to deliver. They get rave reviews. Everyone loves them. Then strain marks start to show. When asked about plans for the future, hard questions trigger defensiveness. Execution begins to falter, followed by finger-pointing. Instead of engaging, the leader becomes more reclusive. This is the beginning of the end.

Of course, every situation is different. However, there are common patterns.

Superstar individual contributor to mere mortal

The early superstar is an individual contributor who made outsized contributions to the company, single-mindedly tackling everything in their way. The superstar is a go-to player and is recognized by the team and rewarded for it. But success means that the superstar's job now changes: it's time to hire, set goals, drive execution, and lead a team. Instead of leading the team, the superstar lets inertia drive their behavior, spending disproportionate amounts of time on individual efforts for which they earned the superstar reputation. They struggle to hire, because they believe no candidate can perform as well as they can. Execution begins to suffer. Everyone looks to the star. Defensiveness begins. Tensions rise. The superstar's frustration rises, and they become a negative cultural force. The superstar now finds themselves a mere mortal.

Executive superhero to mere mortal

The early superheroes are executives who have contributed mightily to the company's growth and success. The company would not be where it is without them. Many of the startup's team were hired by them. The company reveres the superhero, who is a key member of the leadership team. But as the company accelerates and scales, cracks begin to show. Systemic issues arising from rapid growth develop, without a clear solution. Plans for the future look like a bigger version of the past: "That's what got us here...We can't afford to make a change now." Execution suffers. Planning stagnates. Tensions rise. The superhero leader becomes frustrated, recognizing the need for change but unsure what to do. The external pressure triggers defensiveness. In some cases, the superhero goes from cultural touchstone to a negative cultural force. The executive superheroes, who prided themselves in their functional superpowers and ability to lead, now frustratingly, find themselves mere mortals.

The fundamental issue is the same: Unlearning the old role and learning the new role isn't happening at a pace that the company needs to be successful. To be fair, sometimes it's on the CEO for not clearly articulating the needs of the next role. That's on the CEO (and the leader) to quickly address. In some cases, a leader makes a personal choice that they don't want to unlearn and change themselves as a leader, preferring to do what they do best. In other cases, a leader simply doesn't have the skills or ability to make the leap fast enough. Again, the solution is to then change the people. That typically means letting the person go, allowing them to move on in their career. Sometimes, the leader understands the situation and wants to take another meaningful role in the company. This can be a great option because it allows the executive to continue to contribute and learn, while continuing to be a positive cultural force inside the company. It also sets a precedent for future leadership transitions.

Loyalty versus decisiveness—with an audience

Every CEO considering a leadership change will face the tradeoff between fostering loyalty and ruthless decisiveness. This same tradeoff applies to any executive and their team; however, for the purpose of brevity, this section will refer to the CEO. Is the CEO loyal—giving a superhero executive who is experiencing turbulence a chance to grow into the next role? Or, is the CEO decisive—swapping out an executive at the first sign of turbulence?

Move too fast and be perceived as disloyal and uninterested in coaching and growing leaders. Delay too long and be perceived as indecisive. It will feel like a trap, where the CEO is damned-if-you-do or damned-if-you-don't. In reality, it's a balance to be struck, and every CEO will decide their own balance. The one part of the decision that is not a balance: Always make the right decision for the company.

Demonstrate loyalty. Giving a superhero the opportunity to grow allows a CEO to invest in the team, to attract up-and-coming talent interested in growth, to demonstrate loyalty to leaders through the inevitable ups and downs. But the same loyalty also risks over-supporting a struggling executive who has become a "mere mortal," which can damage execution, negatively affect the team, and even cause the company to hit a wall, which in turn can lead the team and investors to lose confidence in the business and the CEO.

Act decisively. The alternative is to make a change immediately and ruthlessly at the first sign of turbulence, without offering the leader a chance to learn. Here, the operative adage is "If you're not sure, you're sure." This approach demonstrates decisiveness to the company and board, allowing the CEO to bring in the next level of talent. But it has risks, too. Firing an executive at the first sign of strain signals to the other executives that the CEO is unwilling to invest in people's growth and disinterested in loyalty, making it hard to hire fast-learning high potential leaders and sowing a fear of mistakes into the culture.

This tradeoff may seem like a private matter between the CEO and the troubled superstar or superhero, but it is not. Instead, it plays out in front of a very important audience: the other executives and employees of the company. Other leaders and the wider company will see or hear that an executive is struggling and sense growing tension. The rest of the executives and the company will closely watch how the CEO resolves this situation. Each executive in the audience

Figure 14: Remember the audience

will have a dual perspective: First, will the CEO make the tough decision for the good of the company? And second, what if that were me someday? Would the CEO give me a chance? If I get fired, would the CEO do it respectfully? The audience should not drive the CEO's decision, but the audience matters, because it represents the team that continues. This isn't a problem unique to CEOs, of course; leaders at every level have to contend with tradeoff with their top leaders as well.

What is the gap between disloyal and indecisive? It will feel like a trap, where the CEO is damned-if-you-do or damned-if-you-don't. In reality, it's a balance to be struck. In between too early (disloyal) and too late (indecisive) is just right, where the CEO's decision is prescient for the company, but seen as fair to the executive too. Every CEO will decide their own balance.

Balancing Loyalty and Decisiveness

TOO EARLY	JUST RIGHT	TOO LATE
No loyalty	*Prescient & fair*	*Indecisive*

When faced with this decision, our advice is to allow a maximum of 90 days to decide what to do with a particular leader. Provide candid feedback. Ask yourself if there is something you're doing—or not doing—that's holding the leader back. Start sharing the issue with a small number of key executives to solicit input—first to help the struggling leader and then, if a change is to be made, to help with the transition. After 90 days, decide to make the leadership change or recommit to the leader. Be decisive. The company needs the right leader, and the leader deserves clarity to be effective in their job, or to move on with dignity.

The decision to exit a long-time leader feels brutal. Loyal superstars and superheroes who played a key role in building the company become mere mortals and need to be let go. Yet, the decision for change is also an opportunity for dignity. These employees helped create success for the company. With that success, the company has evolved beyond them. They deserved to be honored for that.

I eventually turned over my entire team

Anonymous CEO

Our leadership team was close. We bonded for years on the battlefield—customer trips, late nights, offsites. We built a company from single-digit millions to nearly a billion dollars in sales. The team successfully overcame huge challenges, and many executives rose from leadership role to leadership role. They made the company.

Eventually, though, in the space of two years, I had to let every single one of them go. In some cases, they were just tired. In most cases, I had to bring in the leaders for the next phase of the company growth. It was painful as we were going through it, but it was the right thing for the company and, in most cases, for the people themselves. Fast forward five years and the company became a multi-billion dollar company, leading an entire industry.

You never really know, but I believe we would not have made that leap without a new leadership team.

The transparency dilemma

Executives deserve candid feedback and coaching, as well as transparency from the CEO as to the challenges ahead. But there is a downside to the transparency. Even with the best of intentions, this kind of message can understandably sap an executive's motivation and commitment. Yet, the candor is an important part of leadership and growth. For both the CEO and the leader, the situation becomes unstable, a volatile mixture of hope and fear, leaving both feeling vulnerable and exposed.

Real life transparency dilemma

CEO to executive: *"Bill, thanks for leading your team—you've made a real difference. Looking ahead, I have some concerns. You may not be the right leader for the next level, but I am committed to working with you on the challenges. Let's put together goals and a plan, and I'll provide support and coaching. I need you to keep trying 100 percent."*

CEO perspective

Hope: *"Transparent and candid feedback is part of leadership. It's fair to have concerns for the next stage. Sharing those concerns so they can be addressed is the only path forward. I'm willing to make the investment in this leader, who has potential and a great track record."*

Fear: *"Yet I fear that this executive will take my candid expression of concern as a message that the writing is on the wall and will start looking for a new job in the background. Naturally, execution will falter. And talented execs who go looking for jobs will get offers. Midway through a development plan, they'll join another company, blindsiding me and leaving my company with a major execution hole. Now we have to start a search from scratch. Ugh."*

Executive perspective

Hope: *"I've been working hard and have contributed mightily. I recognize that my job is changing. I appreciate the candid feedback from the CEO, who seems willing to invest in my development."*

Fear: *"Yet I've got a nagging feeling. I know the CEO likes me, but I sense worry. And I sure don't want to wake up one day to find I don't have a job—I can't do that to my family. So, I need to peel off 25 percent of my time to start looking for the next job. That means I might neglect some of the longer-term initiatives that I should be focusing on in my current role. I hate to do this to my CEO, but I want to be prepared in case I'm fired."*

This problem is similar to the famous prisoner's dilemma. But here are some ways to avoid getting trapped by it.

Make candid conversations just part of "normal" routine. Set the expectation up front with executives that it's okay to have tough conversations in a constructive way. This is harder to accomplish than it sounds. Encourage leaders to have candid conversations with their teams. Encourage teams to have candid conversations with the leader. Candor is a powerful part of "grown-up" conversations between leaders and their team. The more routine those candid conversations feel, the more likely it is they will be seen as honest coaching, and the less likely it is that fear will dominate and lead to unnecessary instability.

Remove the fear of discussing change. The struggling executive and CEO both have reasonable fears. The key is how to prevent either the CEO or the leader from getting surprised and "left holding the bag." Part of that is old fashioned trust and transparency between a CEO the leaders. The other part is the concept of a modest "mutual safety net."

> **Bob:** *"The mutual safety net is something I wish I had figured out during my time as CEO. It would have helped productively solve the tension and the mutual fear of being surprised. The mutual safety net concept is personal deal with the executives you hire. The deal: If someday I decide that you are not the executive for the next stage, then you get advance notice and reasonable severance. But in return, if someday you decide that you want to move on from the company, you give me advance notice, promising to keep your head in the game and your foot on the gas while I find a replacement and do a hand-off. That way, neither of us gets left holding the bag."*

Set expectations for change: It's a sign of success

Inoculate the team for change during hiring

Logically, everyone on the team knows that when startups are so fortunate to succeed and grow quickly, roles may outgrow the existing people on the team. The problem is that most startup teams first start talking about role strain and people changes once the growth and change happens. That's too late. The discussion needs to happen during the hiring process.

Commit to grow and learn together, but also talk openly about the possibility that if everyone does a great job, the company may grow beyond them. And make clear that this same dynamic applies to every leader in the company, including the CEO.

> **Bob:** *"At some point, each one of the three co-founders of MobileIron—Ajay, Suresh, and I—have stepped aside from our initial roles. It doesn't feel good. It's awkward and weird. But making the change when it's time is 100 percent the right thing for the mission, and for the hundreds of employees and their families who bet on you. You owe it to them and your investors."*

At the same time, commit to every hire that their leader will support their growth and learning that success brings. This inoculates the team for the difficult conversations and inevitable changes down the road.

Inoculate the board for change

The board has a similar challenge. One of the board's main jobs is to ensure, along with the CEO, that the right leaders are in the right roles. When a startup is showing signs of success and growth, a board's natural tendency is to avoid proactively discussing hard topics like role strain and people change for fear of being the naysayer or distracting the startup leaders from execution and growth, until the strain starts to show. Yet, proactive discussions are exactly what needs to happen. Experienced board members can pick up on early signs of executive strain, questioning whether Superhero X, despite a history of great achievement, is the right person for the next stage. Perhaps through coaching, the superhero can rise to the challenge, or perhaps not, and there needs to be a change. This interim lack of clarity is in important time for board and CEO to have candid and proactive conversations, yet it also creates a dilemma for the CEO: How to have a transparent conversation with the board about the executive while not undermining support for that leader and their ability to execute and adapt? It's a tricky balance.

The best approach, assuming that the superhero has the potential to transcend to the next role, is to inoculate and prepare the board for change with something like this: *"At this point, I believe Superhero X is the right person for the next role. But I'm paying close attention to how they do with X, Y, and Z. If I detect trouble in those areas, I'll let the board know, and I may decide to make a leadership change."* This allows for an open conversation, with structured evaluation points, without undermining the leader's ability to execute.

Making the leadership change: Be ruthless, provide for dignity, plan for turbulence

Be ruthless when deciding to make a leadership change. Very few decisions are as critical to the long-term success of a startup as making—and executing on—leadership changes. Make a decision and stick to it, even in the face of turbulence.

For some great advice on how to make executive transitions, see Ben Horowitz's book *The Hard Thing About Hard Things*.

Every leader develops their own model for making a leadership change. Our list is here:

Making executive changes

1. **Move quickly.** Once you've made a decision, make your move in less than 48 hours. Prep the team, inform the board, and then tell the superhero.

2. **Treat the person with respect, and leave their dignity intact.** You owe it to the superhero, who has made essential contributions. You owe it to them as a teammate. Other leaders will pay very close attention to how an outgoing leader is treated.

3. **Communicate simply and truthfully to the company.** The team will see through mumbo-jumbo. There will be shock. There may be drama. Expect lots of side conversations.

4. **Get back to work.** Share an interim plan for how things will work. Make big changes early in the work week,

so everyone can get back to work and realize that tomorrow is another day.

5. **Involve the existing team in recruiting.** Share job requirements for the superhero's replacement. The existing team may know a great leader for the next stage!

6. **Behind the scenes, prepare for turbulence.** It will suck for a little while, then it will pass.

In announcing the departure of a leader, communicate simply with the company, and express gratitude. An example message would go something like this:

> *"Superhero X helped drive the company success. There is honor in that accomplishment and we are grateful. The company's success causes jobs to evolve, sometimes to a point where a different leader is needed for the next stage. I made the decision to make a change in leadership to continue to build upon our past success. We wish X all the best and thank him/her for all he/she did."*

While the decision to change a superhero is a clinical decision by the CEO, it still feels very personal to the CEO, the superhero, and the team. The appreciation for the outgoing superhero's contribution and respect of his or her dignity must be earnest and from the heart.

> *Bob: "Sometimes words do it best. Other times, it's symbolism. In one case, after having the exit conversation with an outgoing superhero, I presented them with a hand-forged katana samurai sword. The sword felt like a proper way to honor a trusted warrior, teammate, and leader with whom we'd all fought. HR asked, 'Should an exit conversation involve a 24-inch razor-sharp steel sword?' Fair question. My answer was 'Yes.' The symbolism and appreciation mattered."*

Prepare for turbulence. Letting go a high-profile, respected executive often creates significant short-term turbulence and affects short-term execution. It sucks. The load shifts to the CEO and to other executives at a time when they need to take on less, not more. And the turbulence is often amplified when team members loyal to the executive decide to leave as well. For a while, the decision will feel like it unleashed an expanding cascade of problems. But if the change has to happen, then turbulence be damned. It will pass.

Opportunity for change: Never let a good crisis go to waste

Any kind of crisis stinks. Crises are disruptive, distracting, and problematic. At the same time, never pass up the opportunities for change that they create.

In times of leadership turbulence, ask the team and colleagues to recommend changes, and to help execute on them in the interim. Having adjacent teams help out can create better teamwork and rewire execution or operations that seemed to be stuck. Leadership changes unleash significant unfiltered feedback that represents an important learning opportunity. New blood and different experiences brings change and new energy into a team. Embrace the opportunity.

The flywheel of leadership talent

While there is definitely pain and drama when superstars and superheroes are let go, these changes feed into an amazing flywheel of talent that is an inspiring part of the entrepreneurial ecosystem, and often good for both the leader and other up-and-coming startups. Superstars and superheroes are hard to find, so other early-stage startups will excitedly snap up your experienced superstar and superhero. For the superstar and superhero, being fed onto the flywheel gives them the opportunity to help build the next great startup.

For the leader, both startup career paths (transcending to the next level or repeating the superstar role at same stage for a new startup) lead to very successful careers for startup executives.

Investors and board members play a key role in making this flywheel work. Investors and board members become a talent marketplace, recycling great talent from late-stage companies back into the next great early-stage companies. The end of one superhero mission is often the beginning of the next. The mark of a great enterprise company is when its superstar and superhero alumni go on to build great new startups. With each rotation, the flywheel gains momentum, building new generations of superheroes and super-leaders.

PUNCHLINES

» In the beginning, leadership is fluid. Superstars and superhero leaders emerge from the hardship of Survival. Then, with Thrival, every leadership job changes with the acceleration, and then again with the transition to sustainable industry leadership.

» Leaders must then **change themselves, or be changed,** for the good of the company. This applies to every leader, including the CEO.

» Transcending requires a leader to unlearn the old role and learn the new role.

» Unlearning is hard. Most leaders struggle with it. The biggest challenges are: (1) reconceptualizing themselves and their job; (2) letting go of the ways they felt they added value in their old role; and (3) doing all this while continuing to execute.

» Startup leaders rarely have a clear view of what their next leadership role looks like. Knowing the target is two-thirds of hitting the target. To simplify it, each leadership role has 3 stages: (1) early leader; (2) growth leader; and (3) scale leader. To help demystify the target, this chapter provides analogies and illustrations as to how the Sales, Product, and Finance leaders, jobs evolve.

» Mentorship and coaching, often from a neutral third party, can be a powerful tool to help leaders rewire themselves and adapt to the next role.

» Some will successfully transcend to the next leadership role. Celebrate them.

» Some leaders cannot or choose not to transcend to the next leadership role. That is okay and normal. Make the tough decision to change the people. Treat them with dignity and respect.

» There are several particularly tense challenges for CEOs and other leaders when dealing with a leadership change: (1) The superhero/superstar to "mere mortal" problem; (2) the Loyalty vs. Decisiveness tradeoff; and (3) the transparency dilemma. Any leader must find their balance. Every decision impacts the company and sends a powerful cultural signal.

» Once you make a decision, act swiftly and confidently. Expect turbulence, and know that it will pass.

CHAPTER 3:
TEAM

Team Survival

In the early Survival stages, the team is a small platoon of warriors who share a common goal: achieve the mission. Every hire is picky and meticulous. The team is made up of risk-takers and pioneers—some founders, some early hires—who are willing to start with nothing and go figure out how to build something. The team runs as a flat organization. Everyone pitches in and shares the load. There really aren't organizational boundaries. Many of the early team are jacks-of-all-trades, fluidly shifting from product to sales to support to engineering. The early startup phase is a special time. It's the best of times. And, it's the toughest of times. The team's shared experience fighting for survival creates a special bond.

The first hires

For founders, finding the right first hires is of monumental importance. And for first hires, joining a founding team is a monumental commitment. Often, the early team shares a common historical thread from previous jobs or school. Previous relationships can significantly help form the early team quickly, but they can also blind early founders to pick the wrong early hires.

How to pick the first hires? Three things: skills needed right now, fit with team, and passion for the Mission. This is the early-hire triad. The hard part is that anyone brought on board as a first hire must have all three. Two of three will feel okay at the time, but it almost always backfires.

Early Hire Triad

Passion
for the mission

Skills
really needed right now

Fit
with the team

If someone has superstar

skills and passion but does not fit interpersonally with team, don't hire them. If someone brings skills and fits well with the team but doesn't have the passion, don't hire them. If they are passionate and a good fit but don't bring specific skills you urgently need right now, don't hire them—yet. You get the idea.

Early hires determine if the company will survive. Early hires shape the product, the company, and the culture. When they're good, early hires bond to form a special team that magically transforms the seed of an idea into a product and a business. When they're bad, they waste precious time and resources, cause distraction and drama in the team, and even send the startup down the wrong path.

Startup lore celebrates stories of perfect early hiring by insightful and discerning founders. The reality, though, is that almost everybody makes mistakes in their early hiring. It just happens. The key is to be hyper aware of the contribution and fit of early team members. If you realize you made a hiring mistake, react quickly and exit them graciously and respectfully. It will leave a painful hole in a small startup team. It will be awkward as early hires feel very personal. Do it anyway. Your startup's survival depends on it.

The first-hires dilemma

Making the first hires is hard. Unfortunately, the common wisdom passed on to founders is often overly simplistic memes of advice like: "Just hire A-players."

It's not so simple. How do you hire A-players when the company's idea isn't proven? When perhaps the startup's founders themselves aren't even proven? This is the First-Hires Dilemma. A startup needs A-players to build success. Yet A-players want to see signs of success before jumping aboard. It's a chicken-and-egg problem. While there is no easy answer, there are some tactics that can help.

- Past networks. Attract trusted colleagues from past companies.

- Sell the vision and opportunity. A-players are attracted to inspiring visions that represent a big opportunity where they can get in on the ground floor. They want to be part of building something special.

- Network like crazy. Find friends of friends. Find colleagues of colleagues. Look for pools of talent that may share a passion for the idea and fit culturally with the founders.

- Use investors and advisors. Leverage the networks of your investors and advisors to find talent. Lean on their credibility to close top candidates.

- Be inspiring, but not delusional. Admit you don't know all the answers. Express your desire to figure it out together.

Closing first hires is hard. It takes work, selling, and the occasional serendipitous introduction. Hire the best team you can that fits the early-hire triad. With passion, tons of hard work and some luck, the early team will overcome doubters and prove itself. With progress toward PM-Fit and GTM-Fit, the game changes. Doubts fade away. A-players will bang down the door to join in.

Sequencing of early hires

Every early hire is important. Every early hire spends precious capital. No startup instantly builds a complete organizational structure on day one. Rather, it's about identifying a company's critical needs at each point in time, and then finding the best person available to fill those needs. Sequencing the early hires matters greatly.

Start the sequencing with engineering and product development to build early prototypes and then iterate. Be explicit about who of the early hires is going to spend time with customers and drive product decisions. Often the product-centric founder plays that role.

Then come the harder sequencing questions. How to decide between hiring another engineer or someone for sales and marketing? What about deciding between the first customer success rep—or someone to find and win more customers? Or deciding between adding HR or finance to offload non-engineering and non-sales tasks from overloaded early engineers and sales people? For technology startups, the bulk of early hires are in product development, with a select few in customer-facing roles.

Don't wait too long before adding the first GTM person. Over relying on "founder selling" can generate unrepeatable GTM signals. The early GTM person helps find more customer prospects, validate problem definition, vet product features, and test early messaging—all critical in the early search for PM Fit.

Resist adding non-engineering, non-selling, or non-customer facing resources as long as possible. There is an entrepreneurial adage that goes something like this: *"Either build product, find customers, or make customers happy. Everyone else, including the CEO, is overhead."*

Another angle to sequencing early hires is to start with hybrid roles, early hires who are willing and capable of playing multiple roles. Combine early product management and marketing. Combine early presales engineering and tech support. Combine early sales and demand generation. These are tactics that can attract more pioneering talent and save money. However, once the startup begins to ramp, these hybrid roles become unsustainable. The roles have to split, with more focused responsibilities. Some early pioneering hires who thrived in the jack-of-several-trades role will dislike the role splits and may feel like they are being demoted. That's normal. Make the changes anyway.

Hire slightly over-experienced leaders

A great idea is to target slightly over-experienced hires—people who were leaders of teams in previous roles but are willing join a startup in a leadership role with no team. They act as an individual contributor to get things done, often serving across multiple roles. The willingness to of an early leader to take on such a challenge is a great test of risk tolerance and passion for the mission, as well as a sign of low ego. And then, as the startup ramps up, he or she settles into a more focused leadership position and builds a team.

Boards often pressure early CEOs to hire heavy-hitter executives. While it is true that bringing experience and leadership into an early team can be transformational, it is a fine balance. For example, is hiring a growth-oriented VP Sales at the cusp of GTM-Fit a terrific decision? Yes. On the contrary, does it make sense to hire a senior VP Sales who can manage 1,000 sales reps worldwide when the startup has just two sales reps and has yet to achieve GTM-Fit? No. Or, does it make sense to hire a Senior VP Engineering who can manage 500 engineers and ten development centers when the startup has only five engineers and is still searching for PM-Fit? No.

Once a company starts to see growth, hiring a heavy-hitter executive can be a great thing. However, during the early Survival stage, hiring a heavy-hitter executive is usually a disaster. Not only are heavy hitters expensive, but, more importantly, they also create execution headwinds and morale problems. They tend to define themselves by the ability to scale and lead big efforts. Downshifting to a small team with lots of hands-on, in-the-trenches work, where there is not yet clear PM-Fit and GTM-Fit rarely works. Many times, the heavy hitter ends up sitting unhappily in an office doing things the rest of the team doesn't yet value, losing credibility and trust, rather than building it. Everyone loses. Instead of hiring them, engage them as a mentor and advisor to leverage their experience, and keep them close to the startup to hopefully hire when the startup begins to scale. The exception is that rare leader who has successful experience in both the early Survival and later Thrival stages who is energized by a return to the Survival days, even if it means downshifting roles and responsibilities for a time.

Team transition: The Thrival moment

In Survival mode, the team grows slowly, with meticulous and methodical hiring. Then with hard work a good dose of luck, the team finds PM-Fit, and then GTM-Fit. Momentum begins to build. The business accelerates. The plucky startup has hit its Thrival moment. "How do we not die?" becomes a thing of the past. The mindset now is "How do we win?"

For the team, Thrival changes *everything*.

Thrival strains the team

The transition to Thrival is fundamental, jarring, exhilarating—and exhausting. It strains the team across the board.

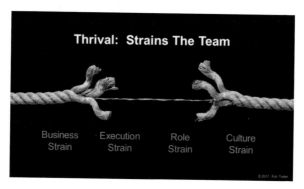

- **Business strain:** Stakes and cash-burn go up. Very measurable goals are easy to hit or miss.

- **Execution strain:** Execution threads must now be synchronized across sales, marketing, product, engineering, and support. Everybody feels stretched. Tradeoffs get harder.

- **Role strain:** Everyone—from executives, to team leaders, to individual contributors—must unlearn their old role and relearn the new role.

- **Culture strain:** The startup must now balance a GTM-led culture with a product-led culture, which is hard on a product-centric early team. The startup begins to hire leaders who drive scale and operational focus, which conflicts with the early pioneers and iterators.

Thrival forces team to rewire

The strain triggers a fundamental rewiring of team behaviors. Successful ways of behaving and operating that have become points of pride and muscle memory must now change.

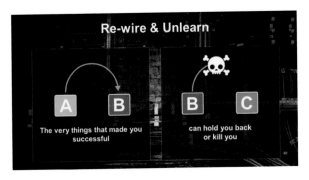

It's painful for the team. Frustration builds because what used to work seems to no longer work. Some will advocate for "returning to our roots" and "let's focus on what got us here." In reality, the opposite is true. Just as for the CEO and the leaders, many of the things that get a team from A to B don't work getting from B to C. And, in some cases, can hold the company back, and even kill it, right at the cusp of success.

Success means the team must consciously rewire itself, and the people on the teams must rewire themselves—unlearning the old behaviors and roles and learning ones for the next phase. It's painful, scary, and often messy, but it's totally normal and totally required. And, in many cases, a career transforming experience to learn, lead, and grow.

Team growth drives profound change

Suddenly, everything changes. The number of people on the team rapidly grows—from 50 to 150, then 300, then perhaps 500 people and beyond. The company's ability to execute is now constrained by how fast the company can find, hire, and onboard the right people. Recruiting goes from an occasional skill to a core competency for the company and every leader. Jack-of-all-trades generalists become specialists. Ad-hoc teams become organized and structured. Lack of process is replaced by some early processes. To the early timers, the specialization and structure feels constraining—even nuts—creating anxiety that the company is losing its startup culture.

Fortunately, growth and team expansion improve execution and the ability to capitalize on the startup's opportunity. A rapidly growing team can build more product, win more customers, and ensure happier customers. New people sign up for the mission, learn, and execute. The little startup is fast becoming a real company. It's a blast.

Team breakpoints: Unlearning what used to work

There's a catch. Team growth generates execution tension, and at times they become so strong they create breakpoints for the team. This tends to happen at roughly 50, 150,

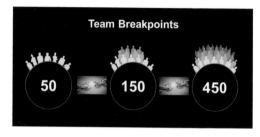

450 people. When the company hits these numbers, adding people seems to produce the exactly opposite of progress. Work seems harder. Communication seems less coordinated. What used to work for the team seems no longer to work. By adding people, execution actually feels worse. It's maddening...and totally normal.

> **Bob:** *"When MobileIron grew from 45 to 55 people, we felt like we went backwards. Below 45 people, execution and communication were organic and reasonably effective. Everyone kind of knew what everyone else was doing. Between 45 and 55 people, it felt like our right hand and left hand suddenly lost track of each other. Silly execution missteps started to happen. Shouting over the cube walls or talking in the kitchen no longer worked. At about 50 people the human brain loses its ability to keep track of all the one-one connections. We had to go from organic to organized. We felt it again at 150 people. Then again at 450 people. Each time the symptoms were slightly different, but the feeling was the same: What used to work no longer worked."*

What's behind the breakpoints? Based upon our own experience, and on the experiences of others who have told us their stories, we have a theory: Breakpoints appear when a new layer of leadership materializes in the organization. The weird part is that this new layer of leaders doesn't magically appear one day. It sneaks up on you. It appears slowly as each team scales up, first in engineering or sales, and then the other teams. Once that new layer gains enough heft in enough spots, the breakpoint happens, and the entire company feels it.

Team breakpoints: What do they feel like?

50 people: Under 50 people the team can self-organize execution somewhat organically. As the company grows, several executives join the team. Then at around 50 people execution breaks and feels increasingly disorganized. Frustratingly, it feels like the team's right hand and left hand no longer can keep track of each other.

150 people: Up until this point, the executive team is the single layer of leadership, operating as a fluid team with a hive mind that acts as the hub for execution for their teams and the company. Now the engineering and GTM teams have each grown beyond 50 people, hiring team leaders and execution becomes more complex. Some tribalism and tensions form between the teams. Measuring success can no longer be simply about achieving a sales target; the underlying metrics matter and help the team make decisions. Hiring and onboarding becomes a core constraint to execution. The question becomes: *How do we keep growing without losing the startup mojo?*

450 people: A second layer of senior leaders forms underneath the executive team, who run large functional or geographic teams, each with significant scope of responsibility. The "real work" and hub of execution is now in this second layer of senior leadership, not the original executive team. Yet, cross functional projects are hell—they now slow down, rather than speed up. Even with a strong bench of leaders, basic things get escalated to the exec team for resolution. Some teams are still small and nimble, while other teams are now large and need more structure, creating a confusing mix of cultures. Frustration builds across the company.

Set goals and communicate them. Simply iterating from idea to idea to find traction becomes a thing of the past. The imperative is now to set clear, rolling company goals that everyone sees—and that will change every six months.

Create an execution cadence. Leadership meetings can no longer be ad hoc. Instead, a regular cadence with a structure becomes a must. Deliverables are reviewed regularly. Goals are reviewed at least quarterly, often monthly. Team interaction shifts from "shouting over the wall" to regular daily or weekly execution scrums.

Everyone together. Purely informal communications fail. Start regular all-hands meetings that keep everyone in company aligned and connected.

Roles clarify. Fuzzy hybrid roles saved money and got the work done. But now it's time for specialization and more clearly defined roles.

Functional teams grow up. Some teams are now bigger than the whole company was 18 months ago. Leadership of each functional team now goes through its own transition from ad hoc to regular weekly scrums and monthly/quarterly goals.

Product releases impact everyone. Cranking out release after release no longer works for customers and the business. Releases now require coordination across product, marketing, sales, and support so that customers and team know what to do.

Culture shift. Product-centric culture must evolve to be a balanced product and GTM culture, which is hard on the early product team.

Get serious about internal communications. The team is now spread around the globe. Remote people feel left out and less effective. Individual teams change work patterns, no longer presuming everyone is at HQ. All-hands meetings go from a presentation in the break room to a recorded webcast.

Recruiting and onboarding become core. Hitting hiring targets is critical to hitting goals. Missing targets—or sloppy new employee onboarding—materially impacts company execution. Recruiting becomes tracked as intensely as sales. It's time to institute a mandatory "boot camp" for onboarding new employees.

Early business metrics. Simple sales target metrics are no longer enough to plan and make decisions. Define underlying performance metrics across every part of the business.

Cross-functional hell. Any major deliverable now cuts across engineering, product, support, marketing, sales. Coordination overhead slows things down, when it seems it should make them go faster. Project and program management become important.

Tension between existing and new. Tension shows up everywhere. Balance new-customer acquisition and existing-customer satisfaction and renewals. Balance refactoring existing product and net-new-product capabilities.

450

Culture shift. Begin hiring operators and optimizers to drive scale and predictability. Creates tension between optimizers and growers/innovators. Instead of celebrating diving catches, figure out how to prevent the need for them.

Stuff breaks, process creeps in—for good and bad. Major blowups demand process. Risk is that process gets overdone, acting as a crutch for poor judgment. Amplifies culture clash between optimizers and innovators.

Metrics become core. Metrics go from messy to fundamental. They go deep into the business, forecasting, planning, and decisions.

Pass the leadership mantle. Day-to-day operational leadership passes from executive team to second-level leadership team. That team does the real work. Executive team job fundamentally changes. (See next section.)

Executive team: Why pass the mantle of leadership?

Bob Tinker, co-founder and former CEO, MobileIron

To help scale at roughly 500 people, we had hired and promoted a solid second layer of leaders at the VP and Senior Director level. But progress felt worse. Execution slowed down, and decisions were getting stuck. Cross-functional issues kept escalating to the executive team, rather than being tackled by the new leadership level. Everyone was frustrated. And worried. What gives? Was there something unique about how goofed up we were? Or was this something others have struggled with? If so, what did they do?

As a first-time CEO, I was frustrated. I called Mark, the CEO of a large enterprise-security startup that was now a couple years ahead of MobileIron, for advice. He was kind enough to help. The conversation went something like this:

Bob: We've added a lot of people, but it feels like execution is getting slower not faster.

Mark: Oh, yeah. Been through that. Let me ask you a couple questions. First, when you were smaller, where did the hard, cross-functional work get done?

Bob: Our executive team. The team is relatively fluid and can sync execution and make tradeoffs. We have shared goals.

Mark: How many people?

Bob: Ten.

Mark: How much time did you spend together?

Bob: We met weekly for a couple hours, plus a check-in call every morning at 8:30, and quarterly off-sites.

Mark: Let me ask you a second question. How many people are in your second layer of leadership?

Bob: About 40 to 50.

Mark: How often do they get together?

Bob: Well, never, except maybe at our sales-kickoff events. They're all in different teams.

Mark: Do they have a common view of company goals, and one another's functional goals?

Bob: They do know the company goals but don't have a view of other functions goals.

Mark: Do they all know each other, and who does what?

Bob: Um, no.

Mark: How do you expect to recreate the interchange and fluidity of your exec team in a second layer of leadership that doesn't meet regularly, doesn't have a shared view of everyone else's goals, and doesn't even know who everyone is?

Bob: Ummm…now that you put it that way.

This was the *Aha!* moment. As a leadership team, we needed to unlearn our old cross-functional connection role. The mantle of leadership had passed to the second layer of leadership. Now we had to enable that same level of cross-functional connection for the next 50 leaders in the company. What we needed to do was clear. How to do that was less clear. Fortunately, Mark also had advice about how to shift.

How to pass the mantle

The Extended Leadership Team: Where the real work gets done

Mark McLaughlin (CEO Palo Alto Networks 2011–2018, CEO Verisign 2009–2011)

Executive teams of growing companies are the center of a complex biological machine that sets goals, coordinates, makes tradeoffs, and solves problems. Over time, the executive team becomes almost a "hive mind" at the core of the startup.

Then the company scales past a couple hundred people. A second layer of executive leadership forms, first in pockets and then across the company. This extended leadership group, of 40 to 60 people outside the executive team, becomes the real brains of the company and this is where the real work gets done. Adding the layer of leadership is supposed to help the company scale, but it feels the opposite. Things get harder. This happened at Verisign. And again at Palo Alto.

The answer, we figured out, was to create an *Extended Leadership Team* (or ELT): a group of 50 leaders, scattered across different functional teams, who could be as effective as a ten-person executive team in setting goals, coordinating execution, making tradeoffs, solving issues. Lots of companies try this type of thing but fail to be effective.

Here's what we learned:

Make sure the ELT mirrors the motions of a traditional executive team

1. Share goals. Every ELT leader, on no matter what team, knows the company goals and the top goals of the other functions.

2. Do real work. The ELT owns 75 percent of its agenda, has real action items and follow-ups, just like the executive team.

3. Spend time together. Create connective tissue between the ELT members.

Keep the ELT small and balanced (harder than it sounds)

- **How big?** 50 people, excluding the executive team. That size team can connect and get real work done.

- **Who gets invited?** The most common mistake is to make the invite title based. Title-based invitations end up imbalanced and often over-weighted in sales, where the bigger titles often are. Better to make the invite list proportional to the team sizes (e.g., 15 from engineering, 15 from sales, 4 from marketing).

- **Don't let it grow.** This is important. If the ELT expands proportionally as the company grows—from 50 people to 100 people to 150 people—it becomes ineffective. Keep the size at 50-ish. The tough part is that, over time, good leaders can be disinvited as the company scales. It's painful. The key thing is to share this 50-person maximum as an expectation at the beginning of the process, and make clear that some invites this year may not be here next year. Some people will quit over this.

Meet regularly and in person

- **Frequency?** 3 or 4 times a year seemed to work. Meetings two times a year were too far apart.

- **Face-to-face?** The extended leadership team needs to meet face-to-face, even though it's hard to pull people out of the field for a 1- or 2-day ELT offsite.

- **Tie to other events:** It worked well for us to tie meetings of the ELT to other major company events, such as sales kickoffs, quarterly executive team offsites, etc.

Every company hits these breakpoints. So, what can be done to anticipate them and adapt? Again, the key is unlearning. Successful teams learn ways of operating that become muscle memory. Teams must unlearn them, and then learn new ways of operating and working together. That's easy to say but hard to do in a fast-growing startup.

Executive team's leadership job fundamentally changes

As the executive team passes the mantle of day-to-day leadership to the ELT, the role of the executive team fundamentally changes. The executive team can no longer be the week-to-week execution center of the company—even though that week-to-week teamwork has been a key component of the startup's success so far. Now, at scale, the executive team must let go of that success pattern, step aside, unlearn its old role, and learn a new one.

The new executive team role focuses on top-level strategy, goal setting, resource allocation and prioritization, internal communications, and rotating business/operational reviews. It's a very different team role. It's one step removed from the day-to-day. Many CEOs and executive teams struggle to let go and empower the next layer of leaders where the real work gets done. But unlearning the old role must happen, and failure to relearn the new exec team role will stifle execution and hold the company back.

Team Thrival: Great fun, great challenges

Very few things are as exciting for a startup team and business than to see a bunch of talented people every month sign up for the mission and join the company. Yet, executing on rapid team growth is crazy hard and fraught with challenges.

Recruiting as a core competency

During Survival, careful, stingy hiring was the right model. In Thrival, hiring enough people to drive sales growth and expand products becomes critical for market leadership. Not having enough people can knock an accelerating startup off the leadership path. Recruiting, hiring, and onboarding becomes a core mission for the entire company, a core competency for every manager, and a key evaluation metric for each executive.

In Survival, a startup might hire 20 people a quarter. During the acceleration phase that comes after finding GTM-Fit, it could be 20 new hires per month, or even per week. Rapid hiring is a fundamental gearshift. Leaders can no longer hire from their past talent pools. Recruiting goes from an ad hoc, manager-led activity to a global core competency.

Recruiting is like sales. A recruiting machine to find and hire talent has similarities to a sales machine to find and win customers. Just like sales needs a sales leader, recruiting needs a recruiting leader. Just like sales needs a strong message to attract customer prospects, recruiting needs a strong "Why join the team" story to attract new hires. Just like sales needs a strong team to win customers, recruiting needs a strong team to find talent and help hiring managers close the talent. Just like sales measures revenue pipeline and deal win metrics, recruiting measures candidate pipeline and hiring metrics by function. It's no coincidence good recruiters are good company sellers.

Recruiting: Red flags

Rapid hiring is *really* hard. During acceleration, leaders are desperately trying to execute on deliverables, often at the sacrifice of time spent on recruiting and hiring. Keep an eye out for red flags from hiring managers:

"I'm too busy. I didn't get chance to hire."

"No candidate is good enough."

"Recruiting isn't giving me enough leads."

Watch out especially if you notice that a hiring manager is green lighting every candidate to just get bodies in the door.

During Thrival hiring, nearly every leader's job changes. No longer are team leaders judged just on execution in the moment. Now they're also judged on attracting talent, hitting hiring targets, and building culture. Why? Future execution depends on the ability to attract talent and build a team.

Rapid hiring: The "bozo creep" challenge

Team leaders are aggressively going after hiring targets to meet future execution goals. In the urgency to hire, they get less thorough and selective. "This person's not great," they start to think, "but I just need someone to do this." So, they hire a B-player here, and another one there. And maybe one of those B-players becomes a hiring manager, who then struggles to hire and decides to hire a C-player. This is "bozo creep." Like an invasive vine, lower performers find their way into the startup and begin to take it over, lowering overall expectations.

Under pressure to deliver, team leaders are often slow to fix bozo creep. Due to the pressure to deliver, they don't let go of even obvious low performers. "Someone is better than no one," they think, "backfilling will distract me from other five hires I need to make. I will live with it."

Some bozo creep will happen during rapid hiring. Anyone who says, "Well, just avoid it," hasn't been through the chaos of aggressive hiring ramps. So what's the antidote? Create discipline during hiring, and help leaders fix mis-hires quickly. For example:

Tools to avoid "bozo creep"

During recruiting	• **Cross-team interview:** Insist on cross-team interviewers who are outside of the hiring manager's direct team. • **References:** Require "backdoor" (or "blind") references before hiring anyone, which means talking to people who have worked with the candidate but were not provided as references.
After hiring	• **Cross-team talent calibration:** Regularly identify high and low performers. The calibration must be done across teams, with input from leaders on other teams. • **Remove friction to replace lower performers:** Create leadership expectation to replace lower performers. Most companies say this, but few do it at scale because of friction. A frequent source of friction is the concern that a leader will lose the headcount slot when letting go of a low performer. The solution is to give hiring leaders "automatic backfill" for exits due to performance. • **Recruit "one ahead":** A subtle but powerful tool is to give hiring leaders the ability to recruit "one ahead of their headcount plan." This means they can always be on the lookout for great talent. If they find a superstar, either make room by adding a spot, or let go of a lower performer without an execution gap.

Mis-hires happen. Empower the hiring leaders to admit mis-hires so that they can be tackled and fixed without defensiveness. Keep in mind that mis-hires are usually the fault of the company, not the employee. Be gracious and respectful to mis-hires when letting them go.

Maintaining culture during rapid hiring

During Survival, new hires are intermittent and methodical. Each team carefully picks its new team members, interviewing for skills and culture fit. New hires are then carefully folded into their new teams, independently learning the company and the culture.

During Thrival, a company might interview 150 candidates and hire 20 people in a single month. And then again the next month. And then again the next month. Without concentrated attention on culture, hiring leaders inadvertently interview for and convey culture differently, creating culture drift that eventually forms distinct culture pockets. The startup's culture, which served as a powerful force to hold the team together in the early days, begins to fracture and dilute at scale. The good news is that, with work, this culture damage is totally avoidable.

Make culture-fit a part of every interview. The demand to hire rapidly causes an over-rotation toward skill-fit. Culture-fit is just as important. Train hiring managers to interview for culture by asking situational questions that draw out a behavioral conversation. Make the pros and cons of the candidates' culture fit a part of the feedback requirement for interviews.

Mandatory boot camp for new hires. There is no excuse for not having a new-hire boot camp. Otherwise, 20 new hires will get tossed into different teams, each with a different onboarding experience, forced to divine the company culture by guesswork. Oracle was famous for their new-hire boot camp, which became a core part of the cultural and company indoctrination. In boot camp, hires get to know the company, the business, the goals, and the culture—and create a network across peers in other teams. In the rapid hiring of acceleration, boot camps are hard to schedule and take time, but make them a priority. Have a regular monthly date picked and reserved. Boot camp should be an expectation for every new hire, including new executive hires. Nothing sends a signal like a new VP going through the exact same boot camp as an individual contributor. And boot camp can't be just an "HR thing." It needs to be owned by an executive or co-founder and have high participation from the leadership of the company.

Culture is the foundation on which the company is built, and the fabric that holds the company and team together during rapid growth (see Chapter 5 on culture).

Embrace change

Accelerating into Thrival creates fundamental team changes up and down the company. Just when the team gets comfortable executing a certain way, it has to unlearn what it's been doing and learn new ways of operating. The team must constantly evolve. That's painful when every ounce of energy is already being poured into accelerating the startup. It's like being on an exhausting, never-ending conveyor belt of change.

Yet it's also a blast. To see people one after another raise their hands to join your company is exhilarating. To see new employees jump in and commit to the mission is inspiring. To see a team face a challenge, figure it out, and unlearn their way to success is fulfilling. It's a profound learning experience for everyone, and a career-making experience for many. To be part of a rapidly growing enterprise startup team that has earned the right to compete for category leadership is a rare thing in business. Periodically take a deep breath, zoom out, and enjoy it.

PUNCHLINES

» The initial team is a small meticulously chosen group of pioneers. Every early hire is critical, chosen for their skills, their passion, and their fit with the team. They set the pace of execution and are the seeds of culture.

» Mis-hires can be catastrophic if not quickly addressed. Early startups are messy and iterative. Avoid the classic mistake of hiring a heavy-hitter executive too soon.

» Sequencing early hires is key. No startup can afford to hire everyone at once; nor do they need to. In the search for PM-Fit and GTM-Fit, start with Product then Sales. Everyone else is overhead.

» When Thrival happens, everything changes in the team. The mindset has to shift from stingy caution to calculated recklessness. Hiring goes from rare to rapid. Company changes drive everyone's job to change. Everyone must unlearn the old behaviors that drove success, and learn their new role. Some make the change; some do not. Change or be changed.

» Growth fundamentally changes the team at breakpoints of around 50/150/450 people. Why those numbers? It's when a new leadership layer evolves inside the growing startup. At these breakpoints, execution slows down, and what used to work stops working. In each case, the startup team must unlearn the past and adapt. At 450 people, the break point applies acutely to the executive team, which must (1) pass on the mantle of leadership to the next level, and (2) fundamentally recast the job of the executive team by letting go.

» For Thrival leaders, being able to rapidly hire talent is key. Recruiting becomes a core competency for leaders and for the company. The challenge is how, in the face of rapid hiring, to maintain culture and avoid bozo creep.

» Accelerating into Thrival creates fundamental changes in teams up and down the company. The changes are awkward and difficult, but are a profound learning opportunity for the team, and in many cases, a career-making opportunity. It's both painful and fun. Enjoy it.

CHAPTER 4:
BOARD

The board of directors can feel like a mystery. The board's decisions (or indecision) can have a major impact on the success or failure of the company, but employees rarely see its members. The members of the board show up once a month or once a quarter, sequester themselves in a conference room for four hours, and then disband

and disappear. They are spoken of as a single impersonal entity: "The board says…"

What is the board? What does it do? If you're the CEO, how do you think about building a board? How do you and your team work with the board members? How does that relationship change over time? If you're a board member, what is your role? How can you add value to the company? How can a board screw up a company? How does the board's job change as the company changes?

Who is on the board, and what do they do?

Board members for an enterprise startup generally fit into one of three categories. The first is the startup's CEO, and perhaps a founder. The second is venture-capital investors who made a bet on the startup, putting significant capital and reputation at risk. The third is independent board members, who are typically successful executives or industry experts that join the board to help.

At the simplest level, a board of directors has just two jobs: (1) governance on behalf of the shareholders, and (2) the hiring and firing of the CEO. That's it. But for venture-funded enterprise startups, the board is much more involved and plays a much larger role beyond the official duties of a board. In this case, the board provides operational guidance, business plan guidance, and shares best practices from other successful startups. It helps company leaders think through strategy, and gives advice on big decisions. It also helps find early customers and recruit executives. In many ways, the board becomes an external forcing function to help drive disciplined execution.

And, just as the roles of startup leaders change as the company evolves, the people on the board and their involvement in the company also change drastically as the startup moves from Survival to Thrival.

How to build a board

Pick early board members as you would pick a co-founder

Picking early board members is just as important as building the early team of co-founders. Early board members are typically investors who take a leap of faith to place a bet on an as yet unproven founding idea. Belief matters—in the founding idea, in the founding team. Fit matters—with the co-founders, with the market, with the risk. Trust matters—the early board member and founders rely on trust to get through the inevitable ups and downs of a startup.

Adding value beyond the money

An early board member should contribute not only just capital but also expertise and relationships that can help the company exit the founding stage, achieve PM-Fit and GTM-Fit, and move forward.

Board members can add value in several different ways:

- **Domain expertise.** They know the space, whether it's enterprise, consumer, technology, or some other specialty.
- **Company journey.** They have experience working with companies in the relevant stages of development.
- **Operational experience.** They have leadership experience in successful startups.
- **Personal brand.** Their reputation helps in marketing, recruiting, and fundraising.

Board members bring their experience, battle scars, and resources to bear on helping the startup. A great board member can relate the decisions and dilemmas that CEOs face, particularly at times of rapid change, and can suggest solutions and help anticipate problems.

Picking your boss

An unusual part of picking early board members is that the CEO and founders are essentially picking their boss. Once a startup has a board, the CEO and founders are accountable to it and get their guidance from it. Decisions about compensation are made by the board. Future careers are influenced by the board. Adding an early board member is a multi-year marriage of four, six, or even ten years. Small misalignments amplify over time. Pick thoughtfully.

Adding board members: Everyone plays a position

Unsurprisingly, everyone on a startup's leadership team plays a position: sales, marketing, customers, product, engineering, and finance. The same concept also should apply to the board. As a startup adds board members, each new board member should bring expertise to the table that allows them to play a position—product, strategy, technical, sales, marketing—rather than having multiple board members with the same skill sets. This kind of expertise diversity is key.

Sadly, this expertise diversity often does not happen in early enterprise startups. Beware the classic technology startup mistake: building a board full of product-centric venture investors, where everyone is a product expert. As a result, board discussions overemphasize product discussions and underemphasize other key topics, leading to poor decisions.

Compare that to a board with expertise diversity, where everyone plays a position. Board members will defer to the expert in the room on a particular topic. CEOs and management teams will get better advice. Here, discussions will be richer and decisions more effective. The startup will become a better company.

No rubber stamp: Some tension is healthy

The board must be supportive of the CEO but *cannot* be a rubber stamp. The best boards push CEOs and leadership teams. They create accountability. They push back on first-order issues and force uncomfortable but necessary discussions. They help CEOs and executive teams grow, navigate change, and make the best decisions. Some disagreement and tension ahead of a big decision is the sign of a healthy board.

Reality of duality

Being on a board of directors has a confusing duality. The board's primary job is to serve the shareholders, but for most board members, the reality is that they answer to two constituencies.

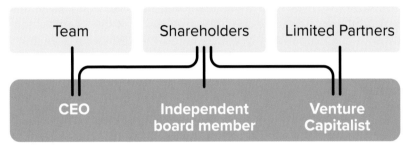

Figure 14: Duality of most board roles

The CEO: Both company executive and board member

The CEO role has a duality to it. The CEO is "in the boat" with the startup leadership team, fiercely rowing daily, weekly, and monthly to drive execution and build value. But the CEO is also a member of the board, with a fiduciary responsibility to shareholders. In this role, the CEO stands outside the boat, watching and clinically evaluating how it's doing.

Balancing the dual perspectives can be tricky for the CEO. But the duality has an upside: switching between the two perspectives can give the CEO fresh eyes on a particular situation. Board meetings highlight those two perspectives. During board meetings, the CEO should deliberately push themselves to look at the company with both perspectives—as a company executive and a board member.

Venture-capital board member: Both investor and board member

VC board members, similarly, play dual roles. They have a responsibility to represent their venture capital firms and look after their investment capital. But they also have a fiduciary responsibility to the all of startup shareholders to maximize value. Usually these roles converge: the common objective is creating overall shareholder value for the company. But there are situations—financings and Mergers and Acquisitions (M&A) in particular—where the duality can create significant tension and conflict (more later in this chapter).

Independent board members: No duality

Independent board members are typically successful executives or industry experts who bring operating expertise that commands respect. They have one mission—represent all the shareholders without the competing dualities faced by CEOs and investors. Because they often come with significant operational experience, they can contribute essential perspective in board meetings. And because they've served time as executives, they can offer practical advice to CEOs.

In the early stages of an enterprise startup, add at least one independent board member to provide an independent perspective and impartial advice. It's important for the board and the CEO. As the company moves into the Thrival stage and beyond, the board will evolve, adding more independent board members, whose only duty is to the shareholders.

Boards can dramatically help a startup

Sharing experience

Boards bring experience to young startups. Knowing what worked and what didn't work at other startups is immensely valuable for both first-time and experienced founders. Board members bring that knowledge, either as investors who have seen many different companies, or an independent board members with deep operating experience. Experience helps a startup to succeed.

Finding talent

Building a great enterprise startup requires hiring the right people in the right roles at the right time. Board members can be critically helpful here, by helping to find and recruit talent. Board members often bring pools of talent from their extended networks, but those pools of talent are often underutilized by startups. To capitalize on a board member's network, be sure to talk regularly about top talent needs during board meetings, and feel free to assign action items to board members and their extended firms on important open positions. Including board members in the recruiting process can help close top candidates. Board members can help find and attract talent.

Forcing execution discipline and decisions

Regular board meetings are more than just updates for the board of directors. They should be a core part of the startup execution cadence for the CEO and leadership team, forcing the CEO and leadership teams to routinely take stock of top business goals, key initiatives, and actions from the last board meeting. Board meetings also become very useful forcing functions to pull up out of the day-to-day execution and measure operational progress, address nagging issues, catalyze strategic discussions, and make big decisions.

Board meetings become a regular point to report execution progress, discuss issues, and—particularly in a fast-moving early stage startup—keep board members and investors synced to make important decisions quickly. Board meetings become a vessel to distill and discuss vital topics. Use the board meeting as part of the startup's overall execution cadence to drive the business forward.

Anticipating and reacting to change

Change happens for good reasons—often because of successful growth. Change happens for bad reasons, too—because of a missed financial forecast, a competitive shift, an operations failure, or a bad hire. When times are good, experienced boards can help CEOs and leadership teams react to change, navigating the turbulence of growth to maximize success. When times are bad, experienced boards can help CEOs and leadership teams react to change, address crises, downsize the team, or execute a strategy shift. Even more importantly, experienced boards can help a startup anticipate major changes, and even prevent minor issues from exploding into major issues. Boards can help with both firefighting and fire prevention. They have seen it all before.

The board as signal generator

Just like the CEO, the board is a signal generator—to the leadership team and the whole company. Each board member is a signal generator, in fact, which means the members of the board can creates multiple signals. If these signals are aligned and consistent, it's a powerful tool to help the company succeed. If these signals are dissonant or uncoordinated, it is easy to damage a perfectly good startup. Use the signal-generation tool deliberately, rather than accidentally. Use it to inspire confidence and motivate. Use it surgically to create change, when necessary. But don't overuse it; generating too many signals can create noise that masks the important messages that should be received loud and clear.

Carrots and sticks

A board doesn't run a company; the CEO and the leadership team do. But the board does *influence* the executive team through direct feedback, recognition, incentives, and consequences. Thoughtful use of carrots and sticks by the board are powerful tools for aligning incentives across the startup, achieving key goals, and affecting change. At a personal level, carrots can involve recognition and praise for achievements, or compensation rewards or promotions tied to key business goals or major company changes, and sticks can involve setting firm milestones for which failure has financial or personal consequences. At a company level, there is one particularly powerful (but very blunt) signal-generation tool that investor board members can employ as both a carrot and a stick: the decision to invest more or stop investing.

Boards can screw up perfectly good startups

Dysfunctional boards

Dysfunctional boards can do significant damage. Dysfunctional boards aren't aligned around the same goals and objectives, often driven by either different agendas or incompatible personalities.

Dysfunctional boards suffer from decision paralysis, driven by different views of the same situation that are unable to be resolved.

The good news: there's a simple test to determine if a board is dysfunctional or not. Is the board speaking with one voice to the CEO and leadership team, or is the CEO getting conflicting messages?

Chasing the latest trend

Board members see many different enterprise startups and share best practices. Some best practices become trendy in the investor community. For example, trends like Software-as-a-Service delivery, artificial intelligence, "freemium" sales models, and frictionless-no-touch sales models can be powerful for some enterprise startups. But for other startups, following those same trends can be a complete disaster. The trick is recognizing when a trend is useful—and when it's not—for a given startup. Some boards get caught up in the hype and push the startup down an unnatural path.

Letting enthusiasm and envy override business judgment

Making a startup into a "fast grower" can create tremendous value and separate the company from its competition. It is easy to let enthusiasm and financial envy override sound business judgment. Enthusiasm is contagious. Envy of other fast-growing startups is insidious. Some startups or markets are not capable of supporting breakout growth. Pushing a company to accelerate unnaturally leads to repeatedly missed business plans and the burning of too much cash, which can kill a company. Reality, calculated risks, and good business judgment must prevail over enthusiasm and envy.

Distractions

Boards can damage companies by indirectly distracting the leadership team to make board members happy rather than focus on strategy and execution. Sometimes distractions can come from the board as a whole, but just as often the distractions can come from individual board members, whose well-intentioned requests for extra data, extra work, side discussions, and need for frequent interaction can tax limited startup resources. Distractions also take the form of disproportionate time on orthogonal requests or second-order issues that divert attention away from core goals and create unintentional noise.

Tae Hea: "One leadership team would spend several days after a board meeting trying to interpret what a board member really meant, because that board member raised so many points at the board meeting. And then they had to follow up on the board member's requests, spending time researching each point and structuring thorough responses. This became a major time sink for the startup team."

For the CEO, running a company requires more than 100 percent of their time. Then add on top the very reasonable need for each board member to feel like they are well-informed and in sync with the company, it becomes a painful time tradeoff.

Bob: "This is a damned-if-you-do, damned-if-you-don't for the CEO. Individually, keeping each MobileIron board member briefed and responding to their questions didn't demand too much of my time. But collectively, the briefings, conversations, and responses could easily use up more than a half-day per week. Cutting back on individual board members briefings seemed a logical prioritization of CEO time, but the side effect was less effective board meetings and criticism of poor communications."

Tae Hea: "As a board member, I can compel an executive to spend time answering my questions or meeting with me. But I'm always conscious that every hour the executive spends with me is one less hour selling to customers—or with their family."

Flipping between fear and greed

One particularly confusing board dynamic is when individual board members toggle between "greed mode" and "fear mode." They get greedy during good times: urging companies to grow fast to maximize returns; pushing for overly high valuations to provide partner-impressing markups on early investments; or jockeying for valuation and allocation of proceeds during M&A to maximize return. But when times get tough—when there are missed sales targets, rough financing, high cash burn, and other kinds of turbulence—they get afraid, which can manifest as paralysis at the board level, overreactions to events, thrashing of the management team, or even holding back a follow-on investment, which, in turn, sends negative signals to the market.

Depending on whether they are in fear mode or greed mode, board members can manifest completely different personalities or react differently to the exact same situation. This confuses the startup leadership and other board members. While the financial logic of fear versus greed is understandable, startups need steady leadership from their boards. Board leadership must strike the balance of not overreacting to turbulence but reacting quickly and strongly to a fundamental issue.

Failure to solve founder drama

Founder drama can happen at any time in an enterprise startup's life. It can involve conflicts between founders who don't get along, paralyzing a startup's search for PM-Fit or GTM-Fit. It can be caused by a brilliant co-founder who is culturally toxic. It can be founders whose company has evolved beyond them, but they refuse to let go. It can be caused by founders who undermine new executives out of pride or ego.

Founder drama is exasperating to employees and investors. It can knock a thriving company off the leadership path. CEOs and boards have to act swiftly and decisively to address it—the fate of their companies often depends on it.

Don't be "that" board member

Startup leaders crave strong board members who can help them build their company into a thriving business. Those board members are widely admired and gain notoriety in the entrepreneurial community for generating returns on their investments. But some board members gain notoriety for much less-flattering reasons.

Parachuting pontificator

Most board members arrive at board meetings prepared and ready to focus on core topics, making measured and focused comments. Rather than focusing on helping the company be successful, pontificating board members parachute in once a month without thorough preparation and then talk far more than they listen, perhaps in an attempt to impress other board members.

Some board members seem to measure their value-add by the length and frequency of their comments. They occupy disproportionate airtime, mistaking volume and frequency of comments for value of comments, which crowds out other inputs. The most valuable board members are those who zero in on first-order topics and drive productive discussions at the boardroom table.

The board's two big jobs

There are many decisions a board faces over the life of startup. The two biggest are whether to (1) make a CEO change, and (2) sell the company.

1) Hire and fire the CEO

One of the fundamental jobs of the board is to hire and fire the CEO.

Sometimes boards change the CEO proactively, to build the company for the next level. Sometimes boards change CEOs under duress, in response to bad situations. But in almost all cases, boards prefer to back the current CEO.

Proactive changes gear the company for the next stage. Ideally, when the time is right, the early founding CEO will gracefully step aside to make room for a superstar CEO—the kind of person who can fundamentally transform and accelerate the company to the next stage. Think of John Chambers at Cisco, Mark McLaughlin at Palo Alto Networks, Frank Slootman at ServiceNow, or Godfrey Sullivan at Splunk. While the success and growth of the company is what's leading to the CEO change, emotions and tension can run high. Naturally, not every early founding CEO will want to step aside, even if it's the right thing to do for the company and the mission. To help diffuse the tension and emotions, celebrate the CEO's achievements and provide for a dignified exit to increase the chances of a successful transition.

By contrast, forcing a CEO to leave because of company duress is traumatic. What causes the board to make such a drastic change? It could be execution issues such as consistently poor company performance, regularly missed targets, or inability to raise capital. Or, it could be the startup's leadership team has lost confidence in the CEO. Being in such a situation is difficult for the CEO, the executives, and the board. Unfortunately, struggling CEOs sometimes attempt to control perception by limiting the board's access to information or limiting the board's access to the leadership team. Unsurprisingly, a CEO limiting access to information and the team is in itself a warning sign to the board, and often the beginning of the end for a struggling CEO.

Making a CEO change is a big deal. It's risky. It creates turbulence. In some cases, though, the board can clearly see that the risk and turbulence is worth it because they know a new CEO is likely to help the company succeed. In other cases, the risk outweighs the upside, in which case the board has another option: try to sell the company.

2) Sell or don't sell?

Boards can decide to sell a startup for positive reasons (the startup is in a hot space and has many suitors) or for negative ones (the startup is struggling). Sometimes the decision to sell is obvious. But most of the time, it's not so obvious.

When the decision to sell is obvious

- **A great acquisition offer comes in.** The acquisition price is very compelling, and the company will be substantially more valuable when combined with the acquirer than as a separate company.

- **Fundamental challenges exist across the company.** The company isn't executing well. It's hard to raise money. There are fundamental issues with the CEO or leadership team. The startup's customer base is at risk. Competitors are significantly out-executing the company.

- **The team is tired.** Everybody has been at it for so long that they just run out of gas and want to sell.

When the decision to not sell is obvious

- **The company is executing well in a hot market.** The company is achieving execution milestones and growing the business, thus creating significantly more value as an independent company for now. Perhaps there's some minor turbulence, but nothing out of the ordinary for a growing startup.

- **An underwhelming offer comes in.** The company's future value as an independent company is much higher than the current offer.

- **The team is energized.** The board and the team believe in the future and the opportunity to build a valuable company. Note: If there are early employees who believe in the future but desire some liquidity that would come with an acquisition, investors may consider buying some shares from early employees to ease personal financial pressures.

When the decision is not obvious (most of the time)

It usually isn't easy to decide whether to sell or not. The board will see company's valuation analyses from the leadership team and investment bankers, but interpreting these analyses is an art rather than a science. That's because valuation is very subjective. It's based on blended assessments of the business—strategic, financial, team. In considering an acquisition offer, the board has to take stock of the startup's go-forward plan (as adjusted for probabilities, execution risks, competition, team, etc.) and its potential value upon succeeding with that plan (valuation multiples, time discounts, future dilution, etc.). But even with all the analyses and assessments, the decision is rarely obvious. The board must rely on its best judgment.

Sources of tension between board and CEO

The board is on your side—until it's not

One of the great things about boards and CEOs is that their interests align naturally—and massively. Everyone is a shareholder. Everyone wants to build a great company and create value. Everyone wants the CEO to succeed. A successful CEO results in a successful company. The board is on your side of the table. It's great teamwork.

Until it's not.

When does that happen? There are three major tension points between the board and the CEO: (1) the next round of financing, (2) negotiating to sell the company, and (3) access to the executive team.

Tension 1: The next round of financing

Raising capital creates tension between the existing VC investors on the board and the CEO. This is because of the dual roles that VC board members play, as discussed earlier in this chapter. While the CEO represents the interested of the shareholders and company, VC board members also have an interest to raise capital in order to help the company grow and succeed, but they also represent the interests of their firms as current shareholders and as future investors. In many cases when raising additional capital, investors on the board and the CEO are aligned, for the very simple reason that the returns for both investors and employees are tied to growing a company to increase the price per share. Sometimes, however, the interests diverge.

The CEO challenge: Managing investors' fear and greed

To the CEO's general frustration, a VC board member may begin to alternate between the greed and fear scenarios. Perhaps the VC wants to increase ownership (the greed scenario) or does not want to continue investing and support the company (the fear scenario).

> **Fear.** What triggers this fear? The most common trigger is that the company failed the "new-investor market test" where the company was unable to get a financing term sheet from new investors. With such failure, the current VC investor's firm is likely to conclude that the company's prospects are fading—even if the VC board member is personally still enthusiastic about the company. Their investor's firm may override the individual board member and block further investments in the company, or perhaps make any further investments conditional on major changes to the company's financial plan or even require changing the CEO. The VC firm may also write down the value of the investment—something that VC board members fear, because it makes them look like losers within the VC firm.

Greed. The reverse is also true. If the company receives a financing-offer term sheet from a reputable investor at a higher price, the very same VC board member and their partners will get excited and flip over to greed mode. The existing VC firm will conclude the company is hot. With a higher term sheet from a reputable firm, the VC firm can write up the value of investment, making the investor board member look like a hero within the partnership. The VC board member will then get pressure from partners at the firm to invest more in the company, in order to maintain or even increase their percentage ownership of the company. The CEO is then under enormous pressure to accept capital from existing investors, even if the right answer for the company is to diversify the investor base by bringing in new investors.

While greed mode does present challenges, fear mode is more destructive. The best way to ensure a productive dynamic for the next round of financing is to pass the new-investor market test by getting offers from multiple eager new investors.

What's behind the financing tension?
VC investors and the markup leaderboard

How does a VC firm evaluate its partners? How does a VC firm show its performance to its investors? The answer to both questions is measuring cash returns on invested capital when the startup is acquired or goes through an IPO. But that usually takes a long time. As a result, investors track interim progress by marking an investment "up" or "down" based on the new price per share paid by the next set of investors. Even though the startup's stock is private and illiquid equity, the financing round serves as a mark-to-market for all the investors. This mark-to-market is normal and necessary, but it also plays a powerful role in generating fear and greed among investor board members.

LEADERBOARD

	COMPANY 1	COMPANY 2	COMPANY 3	OVERALL
JOANNA	↗	↗	↗	1
SAMIR	↗	↗	→	2
BILL	↗	→	↘	3
MILTON	↗	↘	↘	4

Inside the VC firm, imagine every company investment is listed on a markup leaderboard with the partners name next to it. Each time the startup raises capital at a higher price, the investment and the partner moves up the leaderboard. If a startup raises capital at a lower price or folds, the investment and the partner move down the leaderboard.

Example: Suppose an early VC invested at $.50 a share. Due to the company's progress, the next VC paid $2.00 a share—that's a fourfold markup. That progress looks good for the early investor, even though there was no liquidity. Suppose the company later hits some turbulence, nearly runs out of cash, and raises a distressed round of capital at $1.00 per share valuation. That's a 50 percent markdown from $2.00 per share to $1.00 per share, which looks bad for the investor.

The markup leaderboard plays significantly into the mentality of venture capitalists, their partnership, and their investors. VC firms use markups and mark downs as a way to evaluate the performance of their investment partners. Every year, a venture firm stands up in front of investors and shows the valuation progress on their private-company investments. The pressure to show promising markups and avoid negative markdowns is high. The markup leaderboard explains much of the behavior and dynamic of a venture investor board member and their partnership.

The investor challenge: Are the CEO and the team "in it together" with the investor?

When a startup is struggling to raise capital from new investors and the company is running out of cash, the only option may be for the existing investors to step up and contribute more capital in order to give the company more time to execute. The CEO will pressure existing investors to bridge the company to a promising future milestone that proves the potential of the business and attracts new investors. These situations are hard for everyone, and investors have put significant capital at risk. But these situations can also be a great "we're all in it together" moment for the CEO, the management team, and investors who believe in the opportunity. Awkwardly, sometimes, the CEO and team may also jam the board for incentives—additional equity, special change of control terms— just after the new round of financing is closed. Or, even more problematic, the CEO surprises the investors by taking another job saying, "It was just too good an opportunity. I had to do this for my family." In this scenario, the investors rightly wonder if the CEO and team are in it with them. These dynamics undermine a team spirit and sense of joint mission on the board. The feeling of being "in it together" is a powerful force for startup boards to weather the inevitable turbulence of building a company.

Tension 2: Negotiating to sell the startup

During the negotiations to sell the startup, a new tension point quickly emerges: How to allocate the acquisition proceeds among the different equity holders and the ongoing employees (a.k.a. "splitting the M&A pie").

Every company has an existing allocation formula. Usually it's based on three things: equity ownership, the investor terms from the last financing round, and any specific change-of-control agreements with employees. However, during M&A the parties may choose or be forced to revisit the formula.

Splitting the M&A pie

Suppose an acquirer offers $110M to buy the company and to retain the employees after the acquisition.

The question is: How does the $110M get allocated? Allocating more to the acquisition price benefits investors and early employees. Allocating more to the retention packages benefits employees who continue to work for the acquirer.

There are four buckets for how the acquisition price and retention are allocated.

Distribution of Acquisition Proceeds

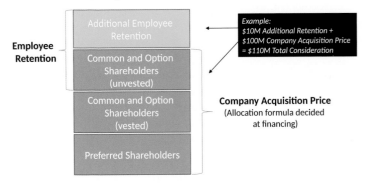

Each bucket of value represents different interests and thus has different advocates. From the bottom of the diagram to the top:

1. Preferred shareholders (usually the investors) who have priority to acquisition proceeds.

2. Common shareholders are usually current employees with vested stock, or departed employees who own common shares. Most of these people are founders and early employees.

3. Common shareholders are usually current employees who are only part way through their vesting. Most of these people are current executives and newer employees. Since these shares are still subject to vesting, this bucket can be an effective retention tool after an acquisition.

4. Acquirers often add value by committing to employee retention after an acquisition.

Acquisitions raise two questions about proceeds distribution:

1. What is the split between the continuing employees and the other shareholders (typically investors and former employees) of the startup?

2. Should the acquisition price be allocated based upon the current allocation formula (which is usually percentage of equity ownership), or should the allocation formula be changed as part of the acquisition?

On the first question, most acquirers care deeply about retaining the talent of the acquired startup and so want to devote as much value as possible to employee retention (the upper two buckets in the diagram). But existing shareholders—particularly the preferred investors who put in capital and vested common shareholders (the lower two buckets in the diagram)—want as much value to be allocated to company acquisition price and therefore the equity owners. This creates a divergence of interests between the continuing employees and the shareholders. Acquirers sometimes exacerbate this divergence during negotiations. For example, let's say the acquirer is willing to pay $110M all-in (to buy a startup and retain the employees). One approach would be to offer $100M for the company and $10M for additional employee retention (total = $110M). Another approach would be to offer $80M for the company and $30M for employee retention (also total = $110M). While the totals are similar, the allocation of value is very different.

On the second question, the simplest allocation of proceeds is based upon the percentage of equity ownership of each of the preferred shareholders and common shareholders. During a startup's fundraising, however, it is not unusual for investors sometimes to negotiate a preferential allocation of proceeds in which preferred shareholders get a larger percentage of the acquisition price in return for a higher valuation or assuming the high risk.

There is an additional scenario. Sometimes the allocation formula is changed to make it through an M&A negotiation in which different players are demanding changes to the allocation formula depending on their leverage. The buyer could demand different allocation in order to buy the company. An investor who has blocking rights may demand a higher allocation. Sometimes key "named employees" in the deal hold a deal hostage to get favorable personal terms at the expense of other equity holders. In general, it's a good idea to ensure a startup's investor agreements, employee agreements, and corporate bylaws are structured so that no one party has disproportionate leverage in the event of an acquisition.

Tension 3: Access to the management team

Board members get most of their information from board meetings and the CEO. At the same time, naturally, they desire visibility and relationships with the other executive leaders. Executives, for their part, desire relationships with board members for exposure, mentorship, and future career opportunities.

CEOs can go a couple of different ways on management team accessibility. Some CEOs prefer that all communication with the board be funneled through them—either to ensure consistent information flow, provide proper context and minimize confusion, maintain control, or just to simplify the CEO's job. Some CEOs foster direct access between startup leaders and the board, believing that the positive effects outweigh the potentially negative complications. Every CEO and board will find its own balance on this.

> **Bob:** *"I am a believer in transparent access between the board and startup leaders. At MobileIron, it was good for the board and the executives, and it kept everyone on the same page. There were inadvertent situations that created painful confusion and extra work, but it was a net positive overall. My only requirement was no surprises. If a conversation happens between an exec and the board, I just want to know that it happened and be caught up on the content."*

Restricting access to the management team rarely works in the long run. During good times, it can work. But during turbulence, it can exacerbate the situation, as the board will want information from other leaders besides the CEO to understand the situation. Also, some of the leadership team will want to share their views directly with the board—in some cases to ensure the board has a full picture or, in other cases, due to concerns the CEO may be over-filtering information. If the CEO historically restricted access to the leadership team, expect the first turbulence-triggered discussion between an exec and a board member to create volatility. If the company has a history of access between the board and the leadership team, these turbulence-triggered discussions are more productive and have historical context.

Restricting access usually backfires with the board by creating a perception that the CEO is hiding or filtering information, which can create a less sympathetic board when the inevitable turbulence hits the company. Restricting access also usually backfires with the leadership team, who can feel suffocated. Encouraging access may create more volatility, but it develops trust and that "we're all in this together" feeling. Trust holds a team together during hard times.

Board advice for startup CEOs

Credibility is the CEO's only true currency

Startups go through huge ups and downs, which means CEO's and boards go through huge ups and downs together. Through all the ups and downs, the ultimate currency for a CEO is credibility. Credibility is a currency that CEOs earn and spend with the board.

Credibility is earned when a CEO delivers, when the CEO is passionate and committed, when the CEO clinically assesses a difficult situation, when the CEO demonstrates real integrity or when the CEO is transparent with the board. Credibility drives the board's confidence in the CEO. CEOs spend hard-earned credibility when they push big decisions through the board. The CEOs spend credibility to push for a big executive hire. The CEOs spend credibility to drive a big strategic change.

Mistakes, failures, and conflicts of interest all burn credibility. Saying different things to different people damages credibility. Lack of trust or transparency completely wastes all credibility----and is the beginning of the end for the CEO. Credibility is precious. Earn it constantly. Occasionally spend it. Never waste it.

You work for the board, and the board works for you

The CEO is hired and fired by the board. The CEO works for the board. Don't forget, though, that the board also works for the CEO. Give the board action items. Use the board to help recruit talent or talk to early customers. Give board members feedback about where they are doing well and how they could do better. A good board member will appreciate the feedback and guidance just like any teammate would.

Decide when to listen…and when to ignore

Occasionally, boards make official board decisions that CEOs and teams must go execute. Mostly, boards provide tons of useful advice to the CEO and leadership team—some strategic, some tactical, some very specific. Board input is always welcome, but the trick for CEOs and leadership teams is to decide when to act on the input and when not to. Running the company is ultimately up to the CEO and the leadership team.

> **Tae Hea:** *"The CEO and leadership team run the company, not the board. Great CEOs deliver great results by following some board suggestions—and by ignoring other suggestions. Regardless of what the board suggests, the CEO is ultimately accountable for the success or failure of a company. A CEO cannot explain away a failure with: 'Well, I did what a board member suggested.' The leadership challenge for the CEO is acting on the right suggestions and ignoring the others."*

Deciding what not to do, in other words, is just as important as deciding what to do.

The board meeting matters

When the board meets, the game is on. It's time to fly—or flop. Everyone is watching.

The pressure to prepare and over-prepare for the board meetings is immense. Newer founders, CEOs, and leaders prepare detailed, custom content for the board to show mastery of the information and preparation. What is appropriate preparation and content? What is over-preparation? What is just right? It's incredibly hard for first-time CEOs and leaders to calibrate. (See last section of this chapter, on preparing for the board meeting.)

Yes, the board meeting is "another meeting." But the board meeting is actually how the board gets its job done. It's when the CEO and startup leaders talk about the fundamentals and operations of the business. It's when big decisions get made. It's when board members see each other. The board meeting is the board. It matters.

Sharing bad news

Sharing bad news becomes more difficult as the company becomes larger. Once the company starts doing well (i.e., Thrival), everyone wants to report on the successes and not share bad news.

Boards want CEOs and leadership teams to share bad news early and proactively, before it festers and becomes a board-level crisis. Boards want time to assess and react—they want to do fire prevention, not firefighting. CEOs and the team earn trust with boards by showing themselves to be accountable and by communicating bad news quickly. Board members, for their part, earn credibility with the CEO and the team by reacting calmly, helpfully, and decisively to bad news. A board member who overreacts to every piece of bad news thrashes the startup and suffocates proactive dialogue. Proactivity requires trust on both sides.

Deciding the right time to share bad news is tough. Sharing too soon or too haphazardly suggests the CEO is discombobulated, so management teams often wait until they have a complete understanding of the bad news and a clear action plan. Executives are trained to present not just problems but also solutions. But sometimes during this waiting period, a board member discovers the bad news from sources other than the CEO, or the bad news gets worse and becomes a board-level crisis, undermining the credibility of the CEO and the leadership team.

The management team and board must react calmly and respond quickly to bad news. How fast and how well they respond to bad news can mean success or failure for the company. This means the team may want to promptly inform the board of bad news even before having developed a full understanding of the situation. In this situation, it's key for the team to develop a plan and keep the board updated in parallel. And, most importantly, to remain calm and maintain trust.

The board's regular job

The board doesn't have to do its two big jobs very often. Because of that, the routine parts of its job become more important—ensuring the startup is on the right path with the right plan, helping the startup execute and make decisions, and looking ahead to anticipate change.

Right strategy?

Does the company have the right strategy? Has it identified the right problem and the right market opportunity? How about the right product strategy, GTM strategy, and financing strategies? Has it properly assessed the market and the competition? These are the big strategic questions for the board, and they should be discussed in depth at least once a year in an in-depth planning meeting with the board. They should also be revisited periodically as a focus topic in regular board meetings.

Right business plan?

Operating plan

Does the company have the right operating plan for the stage of the business and the opportunity? What are the sales targets? What is the right level of GTM investment to get there? What are the product goals? And what the right level of product investment to deliver it? What is the customer success plan? What is the right investment to ensure customer satisfaction and renewals?

Growth vs. cash burn

This is one of the most important discussions for a startup's board, whether the startup is a fast-growing startup on the cusp of becoming a category leader—or for a startup that is experiencing modest growth. Different board members will have different opinions about the growth vs. cash burn tradeoff. Some will prefer driving accelerated growth that burns cash and pushes out cash flow breakeven. Some will prefer more measured growth that minimizes cash burn and pulls in cash flow breakeven. The tradeoff decision depends on market demand, the competitive landscape, the team DNA, and the availability of growth capital. The decision may also depend on investor board member's mindset. Are they growth investors who seek high returns, or more conservative investors who seek more modest returns? Do they have enough capital for follow-on investments? Do they have the patience and risk-tolerance to change the leadership team's DNA for the next stage?

Right execution?

What's going well? Not well?

Startup teams and their boards set an execution plan that combines business goals, product goals, and team goals. No startup execution is perfect. After that, the board needs to keep an eye on how well the company is meeting those goals. Which goals are being met? Which ones are being missed? What should the company do more of or less of? And most importantly—why, and what exactly is to be done? The board is a checkpoint for recognizing successes, but more importantly for zeroing in on problems and tackling them.

Passing turbulence or fundamental issue?

Every company encounters challenges. One of the trickier situations for boards—and a source of significant tension—is knowing how to assess the challenges. Is a problem just short-term turbulence that will pass with execution adjustments? Or is it an early warning of a fundamental flaw in the business, the team, or the opportunity?

Classic examples are:

- Missing a quarter—fluke or problem?
- Losing a big customer—one-off or the beginning of a trend?
- Loss of a key executive—isolated situation or the beginning of an exodus?

Boards bring the experience to help the company tell the difference and react accordingly.

CEO development

Many boards consider it their job to evaluate CEO performance, which is true. Particularly for situations with a first-time CEO, the board's job is also to help the CEO develop and grow. CEOs come from different backgrounds and need to round out their knowledge. Often they are in the biggest leadership role they've ever had—and the job is changing drastically as the company changes. To exacerbate the situation, CEOs often don't spend any time on their own personal development because there's always so much to do, including closing deals, meeting customers, driving execution, refining strategy, and nurturing leaders. Boards can play an enormous role in developing and growing their CEOs. CEO development should be an active part of every board agenda.

Right leaders in the right positions?

For a growing startup, few topics are more important than ensuring the right leaders are in the right role at the right time. New leaders join. Some leaders leave. Boards and CEOs need to be thinking constantly about leaders: assessing and coaching them, looking out for the next great ones. This is a fundamental role for the CEO and the board.

Right culture?

A great culture plays a massive role in company success, and a poor culture can ruin a perfectly good startup opportunity. The board can have a profound influence on the company's culture through their role in the hiring, compensation, promotion, and termination of executives. But the board is frequently late in understanding the company's culture (especially identifying its problems), because the outside board members rarely meet with nonexecutive employees.

It is critical for the board to observe and understand the startup's culture. Cultural problems often presage execution issues but, caught early, they can usually be addressed. Boards must ask if leaders are creating a culture that fosters or undermines success.

Fire prevention

Startups typically reinvent themselves at least four times as they move from Survival to Thrival (see *Book 1: The Company Journey*). Boards have the experience and perspective to help companies successfully navigate the many difficult changes involved.

When things are going poorly, boards can drive change. Good boards drive change when things are going well, too. This is the fire-prevention role we've mentioned before. It's harder and takes a level of proactivity and discipline, but it's one of the most important jobs a board can do for a CEO and the leadership team.

Matt Howard, a managing partner at Norwest Venture Partners, emphasizes the importance of fire prevention over firefighting:

"A startup is like a naval warship. Everyone on the team is on the ship and depends on the ship to fight and to survive. As a young naval officer, I vividly remember fire training. Lesson one: The best firefighting is fire prevention. Don't let it happen in the first place. Preventing small fires is the best way to prevent big fires. Lesson two: If a fire does break out, don't run away from it. Run towards it and put it out before it spreads. Your ship and your crewmates depend on it."

Examples of fire prevention

Helping a CEO develop for the next stage of the company. Hiring a coach. Providing mentorship.

Pushing the company to use leading metrics (e.g., sales efficiency, pipeline, CSAT, NPS) that are not important in the early days but become critically important as the company accelerates.

Thinking ahead to the next round of capital and ensuring the company is on track for a successful next fundraising.

Anticipating the cost structure at scale, such as setting up overseas development before the company needs it, so it's ready when needed.

Pressing the CEO to identify and address smoldering problems before they become fires.

Help a CEO develop a pipeline of talent that will be needed as the company scales.

All that said, if a fire does break out, board members have to strap on their firefighter helmets, stay calm, and help the team fight the fire before it becomes a major crisis.

Boards must also unlearn

As companies move from Survival into Thrival, the board has to do what everybody else in the company has to do: unlearn their old role and learn a new one. The company is accelerating, perhaps burning more cash, and certainly becoming more complex. The natural tendency for the board is to get even more involved in company operations. But that's exactly the wrong thing to do.

Instead, the early board members, who put capital and reputation at risk on an unproven idea, must now step back. If they don't, they'll get in the way. The new reality of the startup means they need to reduce their interaction with the startup team and become more advisory, focusing on their fiduciary role to shareholders. Most importantly, they need step back in order to give the CEO and the emerging superhero leadership team room to execute, while at the same time finding new ways of getting the right information to make decisions and detect early signs of trouble.

Early board members struggle with this. It's hard to back off just when things are taking off. It's hard to be less involved and get less information. It's hard to let go.

Board role and involvement changes

	Survival "Involved"	Growth "Advise"	Scale "Govern"
Mission	Survive to find traction Solve the critical problem	Transition to growth Don't blow up	Govern on behalf of shareholders Help scale
Time horizon	Don't die now	Make it to the next round	Focus on the fiscal year
Mindset	Involved Product-centric Embraces Risk	Advise CEO Growth mentality GTM mentality	Governance Planning Strategic and leadership development
Skills and experience	Product and customer advice. Help on PM-Fit and GTM-Fit.	Experience with growth, GTM acceleration, team leadership, metrics, raising growth capital.	Strategy, planning, operations and culture. Experience with sizable businesses.
Transition challenges	Inadvertently serving as a crutch to the CEO.	Failing to let go of highly involved role in product or operations. Instead, help advise on growth. Harder to know what's going on inside the company.	Getting visibility and information—both good news and bad news—without interfering with leadership team. Knowing when to go public or sell company.

The board's changing visual horizon

When a startup accelerates from founding idea to industry leadership, the board's visual horizon is constantly changing. Jim Tolonen, board member at Imperva, MobileIron, New Relic, and Taleo, describes the shift in perspective as like being a motorcycle rider who accelerates from a standing start to high speed. At the outset, the board has to focus on the bumpy road just in front of the motorcycle. Then, as the company picks up speed, it has to figure out how to navigate and anticipate the traffic ahead. Once the startup becomes a large category leader, it has to focus even farther out, just like a motorcycle rider does on a highway—watching out for what's coming over the horizon. This means planning a year or more ahead and looking for anything dangerous that could knock the enterprise startup off the path of industry leadership.

Eyes on the bumpy road

Eyes on the traffic ahead

Eyes on the horizon

This shift in visual horizon is instinctive for some board members. For other board members, their natural tendency is to maintain the same visual horizon. The CEO and the board need to actively discuss the question of their visual horizon as the company grows.

Advice: Talk about the changes upfront

As startups hit inflection points, the CEO and leadership team will have conversations about how their roles change. The board should do the same for their own roles. What should its new focus and agenda be? How should it spend its time? How should it interact with the CEO and the management team? And how should individual members change their behavior?

Talk about these questions as a group. Deal with them head-on. Be direct about the changes. Look for opportunities to signal that a gear shift is happening—by explicitly changing the agenda, the way meetings are run, and when they happen.

After that, the CEO or board chairperson should have pointed one-on-ones with board members, to talk about what the startup needs from them at the next stage. This conversation can be awkward, particularly if, as is often the case, the board member is a major investor who has a right to a board seat and perceives themselves as immune to criticism. You might say something like this:

> "You've played a big role helping our early startup find the path to category leadership. The company is changing, and your role has to as well. Here's what we need you to do going forward:

> - Focus only on first-order issues, and let go of second-order ones.

> - On operational topics, defer to independent board members with deep expertise.

> - Play a governance role on the operational committees. This is real work.

> - Think about long-term strategy. There is no next round of financing, so be thinking about value creation as a public company. Tune out the day-to-day swings in share price, and the pressure from your partners.

> If you're on board with all of that, great. If not, that's okay too, but the right thing for us to do then is to wind down our relationship and bring in a new board member."

Powerful tool: The board spotlight

When the company moves into Thrival mode, the board will have to back off, become more advisory, and focus on governance. But it will still have a powerful tool at its disposal to help the company: the board spotlight. The board's attention creates a spotlight on topics that focus the attention of the team, just as the CEO's attention does.

For example, the board can ask the owner of a metric to present that metric at every board meeting—maybe in a waterfall format that shows changes from meeting to meeting. What was the goal from the previous meeting, and what's the actual result? What's the updated goal, and what's the goal to hit by the next meeting? Or the board can pick a specific strategic topic and ask the executive owner to report on progress and roadblocks for several board meetings in a row. This focus, sustained over time, is what influences behavior.

Shining a spotlight on the same metric at every board meeting is a very powerful tool. For example, early-stage boards could focus on lead generation and competitive landscape. Or during high growth, the board could focus on hiring targets and performance of fully ramped sales reps. Or during the transition to sustainability, the board could focus on forecasting accuracy and sales efficiency. Or perhaps there is particular problem with renewal rates that requires a focus on customer satisfaction. The trick is to pick the right spots on which to focus the board's spotlight.

Focusing on the wrong spots can be distracting and even damaging to the company. Focusing on the right spots can help the company and the leadership team successfully navigate from startup to category leader to industry leader.

The big transition: Execution to governance

When a company goes public, the board has to make a big transition and assume many responsibilities of being a public company. Of top importance now is the fiduciary duty to public shareholders combined with the quarter-to-quarter operations of the company. The board starts delegating more authority to its committees (e.g., Audit, Compensation, Nominating & Governance).

The composition of the board also changes. The company adds independent board members with operating backgrounds or other expertise to complement the initial core of founders and VCs. The independents bring a diversity of thought and experience.

Compared to the early days, when the board was deeply involved in the startup execution, post-IPO is when the board begins to feel—and act—like a separate entity from the leadership team. That transition can be difficult and confusing, but it's a very important part of the transition from plucky startup to publicly traded category leader and industry leader.

Advice for the board of directors

Balance advice and tough love

Some board members avoid asking the tough questions. Some relish asking them. There is a balance to be struck.

Tough questions are critical. They drive execution. They can lead the company to evaluate its current strategy, plan, and people. Not asking tough questions increases the likelihood of a bad outcome.

At the same time, tough questions can cause unintentional side effects. They can undermine the CEO and destroy hope, resulting in confusion and multiple team departures. Without a balance of encouragement, they can demoralize executives and investors alike, causing a company to implode.

In a way, board members need to think like good parents who know that hard questions and encouragement when delivered together equal tough love.

Manage frustration

What if a board member knows the management team is not making the best decisions? Should the board intervene, or just let the team figure it out? It's a tough question. Sometimes intervention is absolutely necessary to prevent a fatal mistake. But intervention on minor issues can coddle a leadership team that needs to grow and learn how to deliver without a safety net. In most cases, the board should provide advice and then leave it up to the team to figure out what to do. This can be incredibly frustrating—but it's better to manage the personal frustration that stems from this hands-off approach than to neuter the team's decision-making authority and morale.

Boards have a culture, too

The importance of board culture

Jim Tolonen, Audit Chair Imperva, MobileIron, New Relic. Former CFO of Business Objects

Just as companies need to be deliberate about their culture, so do boards. Board culture influences how a board communicates. It influences how a board deals with bad news. It influences how respectfully—or not—disagreements are dealt with. A diversity of experience and opinion on the board makes possible a healthy dialogue that can drive company performance. Boards need that diversity and open communication. To foster it at Taleo, we ran a full two-day boot camp for new board members. We wanted them to learn as much as possible about the business and the board, to get to know one another, and to integrate productively. It always paid off. Take the time and put in the effort to make this happen.

The board meeting: Preparing and executing

Board meetings are part show, part education, part information transfer, part decision-making, and part conflict resolution. Everyone—the board, the CEO, the team—is watching. All the time. Evaluating the business. Evaluating one another. A consistent and productive cadence of board meetings can provide a solid foundation for a leadership team through good times and bad.

Board meetings are the only real manifestation of the board. The CEO needs them. The board needs them; it's part of the job. A productive board is a key ingredient for helping a little startup grow into a successful market-leading business.

Establish a consistent cadence and content structure

A consistent cadence and content structure provide the foundation for mutual understanding, clear communication, and effective decisions. A consistent cadence and structure also simplifies the operational load on the executive team to prepare for each board meeting, which is also good for shareholder value.

Most board meeting agendas have a common set of components. Determine your set of components and build a predictable cadence and structure. Here are some typical examples of board business:

Board Meeting Components

Introduction & Top-Level View	Agenda and the overall state-of-the-business summary. This can be for everyone—or just with the CEO and board.
Focus Topics & Decisions Needed	What topics to discuss and decisions to be made (e.g., approval of annual operating plan, company strategy, new product release)?
Operating Review	Top-level operating results and metrics for each major executive, such as sales, product, and financials. Optional: individual updates from specific executives on their areas of operational responsibility, which allows the board to see into the work and style of each executive
Finance & Legal Review	Review detailed financial results with CFO. Execute legal approvals and board administration, such as equity grants or board and all committee minutes.
CEO-Only Session	CEO discusses topics directly with the board that would be inappropriate to discuss in front of the full leadership team. This can include topics such as the next round of financing, significant executive changes, or a possible M&A.
Outside Board Members-Only Session	Board members review the meeting and discuss the company among themselves without the CEO. This can be very useful in creating alignment among board members. Even if this session is only used periodically, keep it on the agenda for every meeting, so that when it is held, it doesn't signal that something unusual is going on.
Strategic-Planning Session	Annual session, typically offsite, that covers top-level business strategy and overall company goals.

What to prepare for the board presentation

Preparing for the board meeting can seem overwhelming—and a huge amount of work month after month, quarter after quarter. How do you figure out what to cover to create a productive meeting?

Use these questions to set the baseline:

5 board-prep questions for the CEO

1. **What do I need to get done?** What are the key points for the board to remember? What board decisions do I need? What are the key topics we need to discuss?

2. **What does the board want?** What will the board want to know and discuss? (Talk to board ahead of meeting.) Are there any hot-button issues to be ready for?

3. **What is the summary of the business?** What are our top-level goals? What is going well? What is not? Have I fully shared bad news? Do I have an action plan? Help the board look at the business through the leadership team's eyes.

4. **What is presentation and what is discussion?** What is the standard operational update, and who should present? What are the key operational concerns? What feature topics to discuss?

5. **Have we followed up from last meeting?** What action items or key issues emerged from the last board meeting, and have we addressed them?

The most useful board-prep advice I ever received

Bob Tinker, co-founder and former CEO, MobileIron

How can a CEO decide what makes sense to prepare for a board meeting, and what is unnecessary make-work that distracts the team from execution?

The most useful advice I ever got about this came from my former CEO at Airespace, Brett Galloway, who heard it from a former board member of his—a great example of entrepreneurs passing wisdom on.

The advice: Think of the operational part of the board materials as a **distilled reflection** of the information that the CEO and the leadership team use to run the company.

Communicating with Board:
Goals, Metrics, Issues

Distilled and Reflected

Running the Company:
Goals, Metrics, Issues

It's a simple yet powerful mental model. Everything that goes into the board presentation should be a distilled version of the material (goals and metrics, strategic plans, top-of-mind issues, team hiring/changes) that the leadership team uses among themselves to run the company. Boards appreciate distilled insight into the very same things that the leadership uses because it allows the board to look at the company through the eyes of the leadership team.

Thinking this way allows for simple answers to the question, "Should we prepare X for the board meeting?"

- **Situation 1:** There is a new piece of content that **is important** enough to add to the board packet, yet you don't have it as part of your normal operating content for the team. If that's the case, ask why. The answer is usually, "This is actually a good idea. We're missing something. Add it to our operating cadence."

- **Situation 2:** The piece of content **isn't something I would use to run the company** or help the leadership team on an ongoing basis. If that's the case, it's probably unnecessary make-work. Strongly consider not preparing the additional content.

- **Situation 3:** In rare circumstances, providing the board with significant one-off content is justified—usually only to frame a very big decision or when outlining a new plan for the future. In these cases, the content should still be useful to the company to crystalize thinking.

The board can tell if content is unique to them or a distilled version of a company view. The more the content reflects the company view, the better.

Board meeting frequency: What's right?

The frequency of meetings should change over time:

- **Survival Stage:** Every 4 to 6 weeks.
- **Thrival-Acceleration Stage:** Every 6 to 8 weeks, along with an annual strategic-planning board offsite. Sometimes board meetings will be quarterly, but in a fast-growth, rapidly changing company that requires big decisions on growth and investment, monthly may be needed.
- **Thrival-Sustainability Stage:** Quarterly meetings for the full board and board committees. Maybe a separate annual strategic-planning offsite.

What is the measure of a successful board meeting?

A successful board meeting isn't measured by smiles or happiness. It's measure by four simple outcomes:

1. Did the CEO convey—and did the board receive—the top-line messages?
2. Were the right discussions held and the right decisions made?
3. Are the board and the company aligned on the strategy and state of the business?
4. Are there clear actions items for the company and the board?

PUNCHLINES

» The board has a tremendous impact on a startup's success or failure.

» Functional boards can be hugely helpful—they offer deep experience, pools of talent, and execution advice, and can provide critical help in dealing with crises.

» Dysfunctional boards can damage a perfectly good startup—sending mixed signals, distracting the leadership team, or chasing the latest trend.

» Putting a board together is like picking a co-founder and hiring your own boss. Choose carefully!

» As early as possible, consider adding an independent (non-venture capital investor) board member who brings deep operating experience. As the board expands, think of each board member as "playing a position."

» There is an awkward duality to board roles. The CEO is both a board member and an operating executive. Investor board members are both board members and venture capitalists with their own interests. This is almost never a problem, but when it is, it's painful.

» As major shareholders, CEOs and boards are hugely aligned—until they're not. When is that? (1) When a company is raising the next round of capital, (2) allocating value during M&A, and (3) when considering a change of CEO.

» Credibility is the CEO's most important asset. Spend it wisely, never waste it.

» The CEO works for the board, but remember the board also works for the CEO. CEOs must decide when to listen to the board, and when to ignore the board. Success or failure of the company is ultimately up to the CEO and cannot be explained away by saying "I did what the board told me to do."

» The board's two big jobs are: (1) hire and fire the CEO, and (2) decide to sell the company or not to sell the company.

» CEOs should use the board meeting to drive the execution cadence of the company.

» The board meeting matters. It is the manifestation of the board.

» As the company moves from Survival to Thrival, the board's role changes from heavily *involved* (in the early stages) to *advisory* (during acceleration) and finally to *governance* (as a public company). Just like everybody else in the company, the board must unlearn and relearn their role.

CHAPTER 5:
CULTURE

Culture is the foundation of a startup

Underneath every enterprise startup is its culture. Culture is the foundation on which a startup is built. Culture underpins execution. Culture binds the team together through good times and bad times. Culture is a flexible foundation on which everyone in the company depends to grow, evolve, and navigate change.

Culture is also the soul of a startup

Culture is also like a living breathing soul, born when the founders and the early team begin their shared journey. It defines how a team of people from different backgrounds come together and work together towards a common goal. It transcends any one individual. It attracts and retains talent. It inspires and guides the team. It serves as the moral compass for difficult decisions. It balances the tension between company, group, customer, and self-interest. Culture is the intangible but powerful energy that makes a startup's success possible.

Why is culture important?

Culture is just as important an asset as product expertise, engineering depth, GTM horsepower, or intellectual property—and in many situations, it's an even more important asset. Culture transcends individual situations and creates value across many dimensions—execution, talent, teamwork and time. As Peter Drucker famously quipped, "Culture eats strategy for lunch." The reverse is also true. A poor culture creates a headwind to attract talent and can undermine execu-

Source: Techstory.in, March 2015

tion. An extreme version of poor culture—a toxic culture—can kill an otherwise perfectly good startup.

Culture puts mission, execution, and team ahead of the individual

Culture is the foundation for trust and shared values, which allows a group to put the mission, customers, team, and shareholders ahead of everything else. It's the social contract that offsets self-interest and allows everybody to execute, grow, and achieve a common mission. It creates a shared expectation of intensity and work ethic that transcends economic incentives and compensation. Culture is what makes everybody in the company, from the CEO to the receptionist, feel the same thing: *We're all in this together.*

Culture enables execution and growth

Setting and delivering against goals is an obvious driver of execution and growth. But so is culture. Goals are the "what" the team needs to do. Culture drives "how" the team executes against the goals. It creates a shared understanding for how a startup makes decisions, big and small. A common culture enables a startup to scale execution, by guiding the team to make the day-to-day decisions in a decentralized way.

Culture's unusual communication property

Goals get harder to communicate successfully as the company scales. As they get passed down into the company from the top, layer by layer, they get diluted, no matter how well-crafted they are. Like any signal of information, there is a "path loss" (depicted on the left of the illustration). The more a company grows, the greater the path loss to communicate goals.

Culture is different. A healthy and well-defined culture is a part of the very fabric of the company. As a result, culture doesn't suffer from the same communications path loss as a company scales. In many cases, it has the opposite property. Culture becomes a more powerful as the company scales (depicted on the right of the illustration below). For the CEO and leadership team, culture becomes a key tool to enable communication and ensure execution at scale.

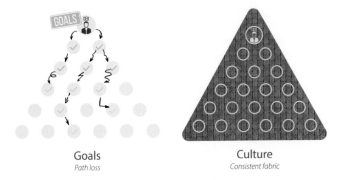

Goals
Path loss

Culture
Consistent fabric

Culture is key to recruiting top talent

Culture also has a profound influence on a startup's ability to recruit top talent. When a startup moves beyond the early founders and initial team, hiring the right superhero leaders will drive the success or failure of the startup. One of the first questions a grade-A potential executive will ask is "What can you tell me about the startup's culture?" Grade-A leaders join a company for the opportunity—and for the culture. If a potential executive candidate gets vague or different answers about the startup's culture, a yellow flag goes up and the candidate will often move on to other opportunities. If an executive candidate sees a clear culture that they like, the startup becomes an even more attractive opportunity.

Culture holds the company together

Startup teams go through thrilling ups and devastating downs. Culture provides the foundation on which the company is built. Culture also acts as a strong but flexible fabric that holds a team together through growth and change. Culture allows startup teams to plow through the

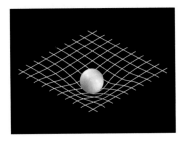

inevitable tough times. Without a strong cultural foundation, startup teams would blow apart under the strain and volatility of the startup journey.

A toxic culture will kill a startup

While a strong culture underpins execution, holds the team together, and attracts top talent, poor cultures do the exact opposite. Poor cultures undermine a startup's ability to execute and attract talent. And extremely poor cultures become toxic, rotting a startup from its core, making it virtually impossible to achieve the mission.

What are the warning signs of a potentially toxic culture?

- Culture is driven by ego and self-interest, ahead of the company and shareholders.
- Different rules apply to different teams or levels in the company.
- Company takes frequent short cuts not guided by its moral compass.
- Leaders must always be right. No one is willing to be wrong.

Even in the most promising startups, a toxic culture is likely a fatal flaw. The responsibility to build a strong culture rests squarely with the CEO, the founders, the executives, and the board.

A strong culture doesn't have to be "nice"

Don't mistake a strong, productive culture for a "nice" culture. Successful companies can have intense, hard-driving, and even blunt cultures. What's important is that the culture is clear, and that everyone opts-in or opts-out of the culture that works for them.

How do you define culture?

Every company gets to define its culture. Back in 2001, Netflix released a famous presentation that defined it this way: "Culture is defined by who (and what behavior) gets promoted and fired. The actual company values, as opposed to nice-sounding values, are shown by who gets rewarded, promoted, or let go."

Source: https://www.slideshare.net/
reed2001/culture-1798664

Where does culture come from?

Culture is magically born anytime a group of people come together to build a new startup. It's a mixture of values, behaviors, decision-making, and teamwork. It starts with the founders and the CEO, and then is influenced by other early team members. But here's the important thing to remember: By the time a startup has grown to about 20 people, *it already has a defined culture*.

Proactive vs. organic

This brings up a profound question for the startup: Be deliberate and proactive about defining and building culture? Or let the culture evolve organically from the team? There is no right or wrong answer. Both can work.

> **Bob:** *"One of the very first meetings we had as founding team of MobileIron was about culture: What type of company culture did we want to have? This discussion was critical discussion for us. It allowed us as founders share what we felt was important, and it allows us to ensure that would work well with one another. We didn't realize it at the time, but the culture outline we developed from that early discussion became the foundation of our culture for the next five years."*

We're fans of being proactive about culture, for three main reasons:

1. It allows the founders and CEO to deliberately define what's important and determine how the early team works together.

2. It allows the early team to tailor early hires for cultural fit—which then reinforces the culture.

3. It allows new hires to adapt quickly, by eliminating the cultural guesswork, which in turn makes it easier for the company to scale.

Don't use baloney gym poster words to define culture

Culture discussions are often frustratingly abstract, particularly for early technical employees who would rather be building early product or working with early customers than sitting in a room writing impressive-sounding words on a whiteboard. We sympathize with them. Overly abstract culture discussions are often a waste of time. Think about the companies that try to define their culture with gym-poster clichés: *Inspiration*, printed above an eagle soaring, or *Integrity*, printed under two hands shaking. No one knows what to do with this stuff. It means nothing to employees.

The trick is to get concrete about culture. And a great way to do that, we've found, is to ask this question:

The provocative culture question:

Reflect on where you've worked before. What did you like and not like about the culture?

This question forces the discussion to become specific and often unlocks a rich discussion where the early team shares meaningful culture anecdotes and experiences—both positive and negative. These form a collage of specific culture points from which the team can define their own culture.

The most important part of defining a startup's culture is that it makes sense, feels real, and is actionable to the team. An effective culture is the foundation that drives behaviors and decisions—and most importantly—means something to the team.

MobileIron's initial culture statement

Bob Tinker, founding CEO

Our culture statement wasn't amazingly worded or pithy, but it meant something to us. There is no right or wrong here, just what's right for the team. It felt like the company we wanted to be. It became how we talked about ourselves, how we hired, and how we acted.

For example, we named "intellectual honesty" as one of the five core elements of our culture. It meant "celebrate the good, and talk about the bad" we told ourselves. This came from our past experience: in previous startups, we felt that we had sometimes "marketed to ourselves" rather than facing issues head-on. We didn't want to fall into that trap. Even though it's easy to talk just about the good stuff, startups and people need to look in the mirror and talk honestly about the bad stuff they see there. It's uncomfortable for the people and the company, but it's the only way to learn and get better. We put it into action, starting off every all-hands meeting, offsite, and board meeting with what's going well and not going well. Most importantly, it empowered everyone in the company to discuss bad news...and figure out what to do about it.

The culture statement worked for us. It became part of the fabric of the company. But, it wasn't monolithic and rigid. As our startup evolved and grew, the culture evolved and developed entire new aspects we didn't anticipate (more on this later).

Make culture relatable and actionable

When describing culture, single-word concepts can be powerful, but often are difficult to interpret, to use, or to take action. The interpretation of single-word culture concepts drift over time, magnifying as a startup grows, thereby diluting the culture.

Instead, take the time to describe what is intended by the cultural concept. Translate it into specific and relatable situations with concrete examples. As Netflix scaled, their famous culture deck deliberately expanded upon the cultural attribute to help make culture actionable and relatable.

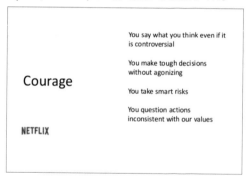

Source: https://www.slideshare.net/reed2001/culture-1798664/15-15CourageYou_say_what_you_think

There is a tricky duality to the early startup culture. Naturally, it emanates from the early founders and the CEO. In that sense, it's personal: the way they lead the company helps define its culture. But a healthy startup culture should transcend any individual, including the founders and CEO. This creates a tricky duality—how to make the culture personal and real while at the same time not shackle it to individuals and their egos.

Cultural moments: Create, reinforce, change, or undermine culture

Simply being explicit about culture is not enough to make it real. Culture is not just be a poster on the wall. Real culture is created, reinforced, changed, or undermined all the time. "Culture Moments" are those moments—big and small—where an action, a decision, or a signal creates, reinforces, or undermines culture.

Some of these moments are the result of deliberate and conscious planning; others happen reflexively or automatically, almost unconsciously. No matter how they happen, leaders need to pay attention to them. Self-awareness is the key: CEOs and leaders need to recognize the behaviors and decisions that create culture moments and use them deliberately. This constant awareness can sometimes feel exhausting. But if the culture is a good fit for the company and the leadership team, the process feels natural and energizing.

Example culture moments

- Decisions to hire, promote, or fire someone
- Dealing with bad news
- Recognition associated with good news
- Tradeoffs between short-term gain and long-term gain for an individual or the company

- How leaders deal with each other, with employees, with customers, and with investors

- Dealing with conflict or issues to where there is no black/white answer

Culture moment: Hiring

Hiring is a culture moment. Each new addition to the startup team either reinforces or undermines the culture. Early hires have a disproportionate impact on culture, as do leadership hires. Hiring for culture fit should be an explicit hiring criteria, just as important as hiring for a particular skill or experience.

Interviewing for culture fit

It's tricky to interview for culture fit. Hiring managers need help. Start by creating a consistent set of questions or inquiries that flush out culture fit. Often these are questions that deal with tough situations, teamwork, and past roles that create insight into the candidate. It's critical that the discussion move beyond "nicey-nice" sayings that sound good in an interview and get to concrete examples.

Another tip is to observe how candidates interact with the interviewer in a variety of specific situations and map that behavior onto the company culture:

- For cultures that emphasize group performance, how much time did the candidate spend talking about personal vs. team accomplishments? Did they seem like a team player or a high-performing lone wolf?

- How does the candidate make decisions? One defining feature of the culture at a lot of companies is how they make decisions. Some are analytical, some are hierarchical, some are experiential, some are data driven. Is this candidate a fit?

- For "go-getter" cultures, how did the candidate drive the agenda of the discussion? How assertive were they? How did they follow up?

- For companies that have a strong marketing culture that values articulateness, how articulate was the candidate? How did they present?

- For companies that value problem solving, how the candidate tackle a problem or challenge?

The risk in encouraging leaders to hire for culture fit is that they can understand the directive to be "hire people like myself," which creates an overly homogenous team. How to avoid that? By ensuring that the company culture is well-defined and transcends any individual personality, and that fit with it is made an explicit requirement in the hiring process.

Culture moment: Firing

Firing is also a major cultural moment—in many cases, more so than hiring.

The decision to fire someone sends a very strong signal to the team. Few things reinforce execution and culture more strongly than the decision to let someone go; it demonstrates what is acceptable and not acceptable when it comes to execution, leadership, and culture.

There is a second cultural moment embedded inside a decision to fire someone, which is how the firing is done. This also sends a strong signal to the team. When somebody is let go, everybody in the company pays attention to how the person is treated on the way out, thinking, "That could be me someday."

Culture moments: Promotion, praise, and reward

Promotions and resource allocation signal to the team what type of cultural behavior is rewarded. Everyone is watching who gets promoted. Everyone is also watching teams get recognized with praise or rewarded with additional resources. Promotion, praise, and reward must be used deliberately. A promotion or resource reward that runs counter to the culture message creates dissonance between what people say and what they actually do. Sometimes, these signals are inadvertent, particularly in the struggle of early execution or in the attempt to keep up with organizational strain due to growth. As a startup grows, leadership teams will spend a surprising amount of time discussing organizational changes and resource allocation. It's worth the time to create good cultural moments and avoid inadvertently creating bad ones that undermine the culture.

Culture moments: Difficult decisions that test the moral compass

Pursue short-term revenue or do the right thing for customers?	Do you take the customer's order that allows you to achieve the quarterly sales goal but that is for a product that you know will soon be discontinued?
Fix an issue or sweep it under the rug?	The startup is in the midst of raising the next round of capital. You find a big issue in a critical product update that is just about to be released. The issue will affect many current customers. If you push back the release date, you will lose the biggest deal of the year, which will lower your financial results and significantly damage the startup's fundraising efforts. Do you hold the release, lose a major deal, and impact the financing, which hurts every employee and investor—or ship the release and create collateral damage with existing customers?
Reprimand or fire a top performer?	A high-performing engineer or salesperson does something clearly wrong. It's their first major mistake, but they crossed the line. Do you fire them? Or simply reprimand them? Firing them will create collateral damage on execution for a major project. And much of the team is loyal to this person. But what kind of message does it send to the company if you only issue a reprimand?

Culture moment: Dealing with mistakes and failures

Failures and mistakes often create particularly powerful cultural moments that test the culture, reinforcing or undermining it. Here are some examples:

- Losing a major existing customer who decided to cancel using the product. Every CEO will remember the first major customer who fires them. It's painful. How does the company react: Does the leadership own the failure and use it as a teaching moment? Or does the leadership revert to finger-pointing and defensiveness, saying things like, "That customer is stupid. They don't understand our value proposition"?

- Blowing a major product delivery or missing targets. How do the CEO and leadership team react? Drop the hammer and fire people? Dig in to find the problem and fix it? Use it as learning moment to prevent future recurrence? All are potentially legitimate responses.

Each response encodes a significant culture moment as to how the company deals with mistakes, failure, accountability, and learning. Everyone carefully watches how the CEO and leadership team respond to mistakes and failures.

Conveying culture

Company lore is a powerful tool to convey culture

Families transmit culture through stories. Companies do the same. Every startup company has its accumulation of cultural moments and stories that become company lore.

Company lore comes from real life situations that reflect the culture. Going the extra mile to make a customer successful. A technical team spending the weekend in the office to make a big deadline. The money saved by finding free desks being given away in an office remodel. The all-hands-on-deck-to-win-a-big-customer deal. Saying no to a big deal because it wasn't the right thing for the company. The favorite movie that becomes an office holiday tradition. The relentless recruitment of an early team member who became a huge contributor. The customer meeting that catalyzed an entirely new product and business opportunity. Holding a major product release in the face of immense pressure from customers.

Any story can become company lore. Be on the lookout for company stories—good and bad—that can help transmit culture. They become part of the company's cultural identity. They enable the CEO to communicate the culture to every current and future employee.

Culture can't be a mystery—talk about it

Don't make culture a mystery that new hires must observe and divine over time. Leaving new hires to figure culture out slows down execution and risks creating fractured micro-cultures. Be explicit. Make culture part of new hire onboarding. Make it part of the introduction for every all-hands. Talk about culture as part of executive offsites. Make culture just as much a part of the company's active dialogue as discussions about product and customers. Being explicit helps make culture a fabric that holds everything together.

Even seemingly logistical things can influence culture

Some things that seem logistical in nature influence culture.

- **Work expectations.** What time do the leaders show up in the office? What time do they leave? What happens over the weekend?

- **Office space.** The physical layout of office space influences how people work together. Is the space open and collaborative, or is everyone in their own space with privacy?

- **Family and social assumptions.** Is every Friday a happy hour because the team is mostly young and single? Or do people head home to be with their families? Are there regular social events? What is the expectation for attendance?

- **Scheduling bias.** Are company meetings set only in the time zone of the headquarters team, or do meetings accommodate a geographic and globally distributed team?

Conveying culture during rapid growth

The shift to rapid growth is a dangerous cultural moment. A startup culture can fracture or dissolve when lots of new hires suddenly join the team and are spread around the globe. How can a startup maintain and convey culture during fast growth?

Responsibility rests squarely with the leaders to convey culture during rapid growth. In our experience, several strategies can help:

1. **Interview for culture fit.** This seems basic, but it's usually poorly done. Train hiring managers to interview for not just technical or domain skills but also mindset and culture fit.

2. **Run a new-hire boot camp.** As we explained in Chapter 3, there's no excuse for not doing this. Define the culture during boot camp. Create situations in the sessions that introduce new hires into the culture.

3. **Emphasize culture and use it.** Talk about culture as a leadership team. Talk about culture in all-hands meetings. Talk about culture with the team as part of normal every day operations. Refer to the culture and use it when making decisions or dealing with difficult situations.

4. **Fire for non-culture fit.** During rapid growth, hiring mistakes happen. If a team member becomes a poor culture fit, a leader must act, or that person will undermine and fracture the culture for everyone else. Plus, nothing reinforces culture more than firing someone who doesn't fit.

Not every cultural leader shows up on the org chart

The CEO, founders, and top leaders all play pivotal roles in defining a company's culture. However, there are less obvious culture leaders who don't show up in the hierarchy of the company's organization chart.

The cultural importance of the office manager

Bob Tinker, MobileIron

In the early days of a startup, after the CEO and founders,

who is the most powerful influencer of startup culture? The office manager.

Why? The office manager is the glue that holds the early startup together. The office manager takes care of the company and the people. The office manager is the one person every employee interacts with on a regular basis, every new employee gets guidance from, and every candidate meets. The office manager keeps the wheels on the little startup wagon when it's wobbly and bumpy.

Back in the early days of MobileIron, I didn't understand this at all. We just got lucky. Only in the rearview mirror did I realize how key our office manager was to the formation of our culture.

The story: MobileIron had ten people. We needed to move into our first sublease, and as part of that, we planned to hire an office manager to take care of the office, the people, some scheduling, and some HR. We interviewed several people, and it came down to two candidates.

- **Candidate A:** Had previous tech-office manager experience, was very organized, had good execution, and was very nice. But was kind of stiff and a little dour.

- **Candidate B:** Had no tech experience and had been office manager for a tugboat firm in Oakland. She got things done. She had great attitude, was positive, and was curious to learn. But she had no tech startup experience.

We went with B. Her name was Angie. Little did I know just how profoundly Angie's positive demeanor, attitude, and get-it-done execution would pervade our culture.

Angie did everything from HR and payroll to ordering laptops, setting up interviews, and ensuring we got fed. She strengthened and reinforced our culture from the very beginning. She was able to move mountains and everyone respected her. Her attitude and culture pervaded the company. She also dished out tough love when necessary, even posting this hilarious sign in the kitchen:

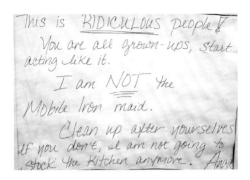

This is RIDICULOUS people!
You are all grown-ups, start
acting like it.
I am NOT the
Mobile Iron maid.
Clean up after yourselves!
If you don't, I am not going to
stock the kitchen anymore. Angie

Angie was a linchpin in the culture. Ten years later, she is still part of the company. Thank you, Angie.

Cultural inertia

The bad news is that culture can also hold a company back. While a strong culture is a positive feature of a great startup, it has to evolve as the company moves from stage to stage, or changes strategy. If culture is inert and fixed, it becomes a straitjacket.

Culture has an inertia to it. Cultural inertia is a powerful force that helps startup teams plow ahead and overcome challenges, but that same cultural inertia unchecked can be a powerful obstacle. Phrases like "This is what got us here" or "This is how we are" signal a cultural mindset that's rigid and resists evolution. Sometimes the rigidity is subtle—company behaviors or invisible habits that camouflage a subconscious dogma. In some cases, cultural inertia is the single biggest factor in preventing the transition from Survival to Thrival. Successful startups evolve their culture. Evolving culture and overcoming cultural inertia can be surprisingly slow, requiring hard work and significant focus from a CEO and leadership team.

Culture is an evolving foundation

Successful companies recognize that their cultures have to evolve as the company changes.

Big cultural shifts: Expect them, enable them

Evolving culture is just as important as setting the initial culture. As a company grows, new aspects of the culture evolve unexpectedly, and some cultural values need to be tune—or, in some cases, flat-out changed. The hard part is to figure out what should stay and what should go. CEOs, leadership teams, and founders should pay close attention to when and how culture changes or should change, Everybody in the company needs to work on this—change has to be enabled, not resisted. But this won't be easy, especially for early employees who enthusiastically embraced the early culture.

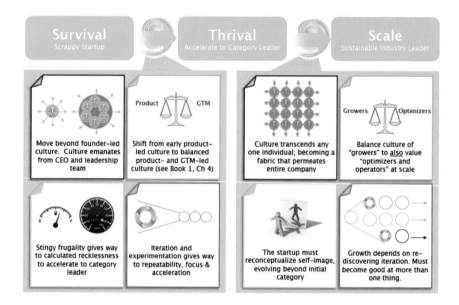

Making changes to culture: Discuss them, be explicit

Culture changes often sneak up on a team gradually. Noticing it and acting on it requires stepping back periodically from day-to-day execution and specifically focus on culture changes that are happening or need to happen.

A powerful exercise for a company is to periodically ask: *"What are the aspects of our culture that we haven't defined? What needs to be tuned? What about our culture isn't working and needs to be changed?"*

Unanticipated aspects of culture evolve

Bob: *"The culture statement that we developed during the early days at MobileIron held true for our first four to five years. Over time, additional aspects of our culture developed that we did not anticipate, some of which became fundamental to who we became as a company. A new cultural aspect evolved organically: tenacity. We added it and a descriptor to our culture statement."*

Tenacity
Drive to action, never give up, and deliver results

Culture elements that worked now need to be tuned

Bob: *"Intellectual honesty was one of the most important early aspects of our culture. Later, as the company grew, it wasn't clear to everyone what that meant. In some cases, we found the concept was being used as justification to be an a-hole. That obviously wasn't the intent. So we made our definition more proscriptive: 'Intellectual honesty: Celebrate the good. Talk about the bad. Be constructive." I initially wanted to use 'Don't be an asshole' instead of 'Be constructive,' but we decided we didn't want the word on every conference room wall."*

Intellectual Honesty
Celebrate the good. Talk about the bad. Be constructive.

Early cultural pillar that no longer works

Bob: *"'Frugality' was part of our culture statement in the early days. We believed frugality was like exercise—regular* *practice of it would make a startup stronger. A spend-freely environment creates sloppiness and weakness. However, as we grew and began accelerating, we would still occasionally be 'penny-wise and pound-foolish,' and that got in our way. The team recognized it and pushed me to make a change. Interestingly, I was opposed to the change, but the team was right. We removed 'Frugality' from our culture statement and replaced it with this: 'Practicality: Exercise good judgment. Balance near and long-term.'"*

Practicality
Exercise good judgment. Balance near and long-term.

Hard topics on culture

Transparency is great...it just doesn't last

The members of early-stage teams need transparency in order to succeed. Transparency is empowering. Many teams start out with transparency as an explicit element of their corporate culture. Transparency bonds the team, aligns execution, fosters trust, brings issues to the table, and gets everyone on the same page. Hang onto it as long as you can.

And then, at some point as the company scales, complete transparency becomes harder and harder. Transparency requires confidentiality, trust, and discretion, particularly in a late-stage startup that has big competitors and analysts vying for inside information. In a big organization, unfortunately, important information shared in the spirit of transparency will often leak. This sucks. It hurts personally. You desperately want to share and maintain transparency and trust everyone to be an adult—and then someone blows it. Ultimately, you have to prioritize execution over transparency. This usually happens when (1) a company becomes a meaningful market player, and its market and competitors are looking for dirt or insight that can be used against it; or (2) industry analysts and investors are looking for privileged information that can give them an advantage.

Bob: *"I remember vividly when an outside analyst cited our performance numbers almost exactly as they had been shared less than a week before in a company all-hands."*

Advice: (1) Hang onto transparency as long as you can; (2) don't completely "shut off" transparency, just dial it back; (3) share as much information as widely as you can, but maintain a smaller circle that gets the full story.

Loss of intimacy

Startup work is intimate. The people on an early team know everything about one another at work—and sometimes outside of work. That's the nature of intense bonding experiences. But as a company scales, its numbers grow, and jobs get specialized. This means less intimacy. There will come a day when you see someone walking down the hall, and you won't know their name or what they do. That's a pivotal moment, and it will feel wrong. That's why you'll often hear early employees at a startup say, "Things aren't like they used to be." The loss is real, and they have a right to feel sad about it—but it is offset by company success.

Integrating another culture via acquisition

Later stage startups will often do acquisitions of a team or a product. Those acquired teams and products come with their own culture. The success or failure of an acquisition often depends on how well cultures are merged. How much should a team be left alone? How much should it be integrated? How to merge the cultures? Which one should dominate?

Subcultures: Some are okay

Every company has its overall company culture. However, as a company grows, the larger functional teams will begin to develop their own subcultures. Sales will have one. Engineering will one. Some degree of subcultures is okay and totally normal. What would not be okay is a subculture that somehow undermines the overall culture. Contrarian subcultures spawn politics and strife, and they damage execution. Often, a contrarian subculture is rooted with the leader of that team. If that is happening, address it immediately. Subcultures can have different characteristics, but they must be supportive of the overall company culture.

Culture is the foundation for success

Culture is the foundation on which every startup is built. Culture becomes the soul of the company. It guides the company. It brings the company together. It binds the team together in good times and bad. Culture is a common set of behaviors and values that arise anytime a group of people are on a shared mission. It's a foundation that can be built purposefully and deliberately or organically. Every decision and action can be a cultural moment to reinforce, evolve, or undermine culture.

Culture is not a monolithic and rigid foundation made of stone; culture evolves, like a fabric that stretches to enable change, while still binding the company together. Culture is just as important asset, perhaps more so, than technology, team, or intellectual property. Culture transcends strategy, becoming the very foundation for success. The culture is the company.

PUNCHLINES

» Culture is the soul of the startup. By the time a team has 20 people, it has a culture. The question is be proactive or organic? We prefer proactive. Define and direct the culture you want to have.

» Culture holds a team together during good times and bad. It is the foundation for growth and execution. Culture is just as much of an asset as technology, talent, or GTM.

» The trick about defining culture is to use real words and concepts that are concrete, mean something to the team, and are actionable. Don't let culture be defined too abstractly or conceptually. A powerful question to help catalyze a concrete culture discussion is "Tell me about past companies you have worked for and the culture—what did you like and not like?"

» Whenever culture is defined, reinforced, changed, or undermined, for good for bad, you have a cultural moment. Cultural moments happen all the time—hiring, firing, promotions, and tough decisions. Be deliberate, not accidental, about them.

» Culture is a fundamental element of execution and a powerful tool for the CEO. Culture pervades the company and is the one tool that doesn't dilute for the CEO as the team grows.

» Culture is a foundation that holds the company together, but it cannot be rigid and dogmatic. Culture must evolve over time in response to company changes.

» The culture is the company.

CLOSING THOUGHTS

Building a startup is a blast. It's the opportunity to make a difference. It's the opportunity to build something from nothing. It's an energizing opportunity to learn. And for those lucky startups who unlock growth, growth is really fun. Growth is validation. Growth creates value for the company, the people, and the investors.

This book was driven by a single question: **Why is building a startup so hard on the people?**

Surviving is hard. Being a CEO, a leader, or a team member in an early stage startup fighting to survive is incredibly stressful. Can we iterate to find GTM-Fit before we run out of cash and die? Can we hire the right talent even though we're not yet proven? And for first timers, how do we know if we did the right thing if we've never done this before?

And then, for the lucky startups who unlock growth, growth is surprisingly hard on the people at a professional and personal level. Over a coffee or drink, ask any leader of a fast-growing startup leader in Thrival model about their startup journey, and they will tell you just how hard it is on them personally and on the rest of the team. The look in their eye will shift back and forth between an energized sparkle and a weary wisdom. Why is that?

The first reason: Growth changes everyone's jobs from the CEO to the leaders to the team to the board. How they work, communicate, behave. As a result, **everyone must change themselves, or be changed,** all while executing in the crazy intensity of a fast-growing startup.

The second reason: There is frustratingly little institutional knowledge passed down in the entrepreneurial ecosystem to help startup leaders **understand how their job changes** as the company changes, and as a result, how they must **change themselves as a leader**.

What does this mean for the entrepreneur? It means that, ironically, the very things that make a startup leader successful in one stage

often become the very things that holds them back or potentially kills them in the next stage.

Unlearning is the key

So much of building a startup is learning. Ironically, we rarely stop to think about what we need to unlearn. Unlearning what used to work and learning what will work for the next stage. Unlearning the old role and learning the new role. Unlearning old behaviors that drove success in the previous stage, and learning new behaviors that are required success for the next. Unlearning is the ability for a person to rewire themselves to meet the needs of what's next, and without unlearning, leaders and companies will stall.

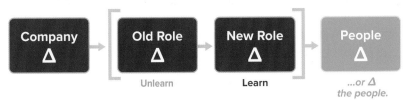

Unlearning can be unpleasant because it means going from feeling competent to incompetent. Unlearning can foster insecurity, creating questions of self-worth as a leader lets go of the ways they perceive they added value in the past. Yet unlearning is exactly what a startup leader must do. It is the key to a leader rewiring themselves in order to adapt to next stage. It's hard—like rewiring an airplane while in flight. In some cases, leaders prefer not to, or are unable to, unlearn the old role and learn the new. In that case, the only choice is to then change the people. However, those leaders who can unlearn the old and learn the new after overcoming their feelings of insecurity can experience significant professional and personal growth.

Anticipate the next role

Each leader's job and required behaviors are different at each stage. Each leadership job changes drastically as the company changes, even though the title didn't change. A leader's job is one role in the scary Survival stage, another role during the high growth acceleration phase, and a third role in the scale phase when wrestling with the transition to sustainable industry leader.

The trick is to anticipate and understand how you and your team's leadership jobs change. What is required to succeed at the current and next stage? How does it differ from the last role and why?

For each leadership role, we find metaphors from history, military and pop culture helpful to characterize how the roles change and get a feel for what must be unlearned and learned. We found these metaphors helpful to understand role changes as a startup grows. Each of these roles and metaphors are discussed in detail in their respective chapters.

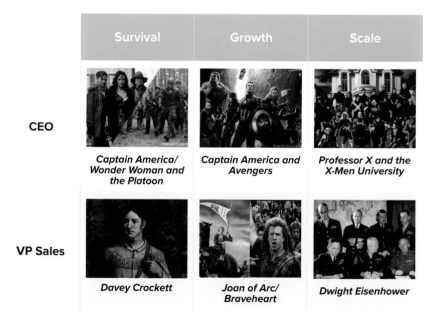

	Survival	Growth	Scale
CEO	Captain America/ Wonder Woman and the Platoon	Captain America and Avengers	Professor X and the X-Men University
VP Sales	Davey Crockett	Joan of Arc/ Braveheart	Dwight Eisenhower

VP Engineering

Frontier craftsman

General contractor

Campus developer

CFO

Supply Quartermaster

Airplane Navigator

Copilot

Everyone in the company, including the CEO and board, must adapt to the new roles. Adapt and evolve to the future. Each leader's future depends on it. The company's fate depends on it.

Change or be changed

Adapting and evolving to the next stage is not easy. Great and loyal people for one stage may unfortunately be the wrong person for the next stage. And it applies to everybody in the company, even the founders and CEO, who in some cases must step aside for the good of the company and the mission. Superheroes become mere mortals. It's hard.

Change is a byproduct of success, even if it doesn't feel like it. Success drives enormous changes across the company and the people. The way the company operate will change. The way teams operate will change. People will change. Some early employees thrive on the change, adapting to each new role. Some will not adapt, forcing a change, which is hard, but it brings in new energy with new skills, new ideas, and new perspectives. Change is healthy.

Culture is the foundation

Underneath every enterprise startup is its culture. Culture is the foundation on which a startup is built. Culture underpins execution. Culture binds the team together through good times and bad times. It transcends any one individual. It attracts and retains talent. It inspires and guides the team. It serves as the moral compass for difficult decisions. It balances the tension between company, group, customer, and self-interest. Culture is the intangible but powerful energy that makes a startup's success possible. Culture is a flexible foundation on which everyone in the company depends to grow, evolve, and navigate change.

Culture is a foundation that can be built purposefully and deliberately or organically. Every decision and action is an opportunity to reinforce, evolve, or undermine culture. Culture is not a monolithic and rigid foundation made of stone, rather culture evolves, like a fabric that stretches to enable change, while still binding the company together. Just as the team must evolve, so must the culture.

Culture transcends strategy, becoming the very foundation for success. The culture is the company.

The personal journey

Building a startup is simultaneously energizing and terrifying at both a professional and personal level, yet it is a spectacular learning experience. Be open-minded and reach inside yourself to become self-aware. Learn to recognize the habits, reflexes, and fundamental behaviors that were conditioned by past successes. Anticipate the next leadership role and stretch yourself to play up to the role. Be willing to unlearn that which made you successful and face the insecurity that comes along with it. It's hard. Really hard. Yet, everyone has faced and will continue to face the same challenges together. You, us, and every leader that contributed an anecdote to this project, have had many successes and just as many failures along their personal journey. It's how we learn. It's how we unlearn. It's how we make a difference. We are all in this together.

Good luck! Survive well. Thrive well.

Bob & Tae Hea